Unveiling Weddings

GETTING THE MOST OUT OF YOUR ENGAGEMENT FROM YES TO I DO!

A COLLECTION OF STORIES & INSIGHT

BY REBECCA SACERDOTI, PH.D.,
& TASHA JACKSON FITZGERALD, M.A.

TABLE OF CONTENTS

Foreword   5
Introduction   9

CHAPTER ONE

I Am Engaged, But I Feel a Bit Zany   13

Emotional Myths
The Actual Reality: An Emotional Rollercoaster
The Actual Reality: An Emotional Tug-of-War

CHAPTER TWO

Becoming a Bridal Buddha &
Beating the Beast of Bridezilla   23

Strategies for Becoming a Bridal Buddha
Strategies for Beating the Beast of Bridezilla

CHAPTER THREE

The Dreaded (or Perhaps Desirous) Process of
Planning   49

Choosing Your "Planning Principle" –
    Enjoy the Adventure, Let It Be Easy
Decisions, Decisions, Decisions—
    Beating Out the "Shoulds, Musts & Have-To's"
Creating a Stress-Free Zone

CHAPTER FOUR

Relationships: Managing the 3 F's Without
Letting the "F" Word Sneak In   75

Digging Up the Dirt—Reliving Roles & Readjusting to New
    Ones
The 1st F—Your Fiancé
The 2nd F—Family
The 3rd F—Friends
The Fix—Finding Empathy

CHAPTER FIVE

Your (Un)-dentity: Uncovering, Understanding, & Ultimately Unveiling You   129

Uncover: Peeling Back the Core of the Cake
Understand: Patterns of the Past & Their Impact on the
    Present
Unveiling You & Your Worth

CHAPTER SIX

The Finale—Supporting Yourself on the Big Day   153

Your Emotional Game Plan
Bad Behavior—How To Manage the Rude, Ridiculous, and
    Absurd
Your Metaphorical Anchor

CHAPTER SEVEN

After the Fanfare: Post-Wedding Blues   165

Married And I Can't Get Up
It's A Wrap
Postscript
Acknowledgements
Appendix

FOREWORD

As two professional psychotherapists who make a living helping individuals navigate their major life transitions, we were struck by the fact that getting married was even more complicated than we originally thought it would be. During our own wedding planning processes, we found ourselves searching for a better understanding of what was going on inside—the extreme emotional states, the subtle cultural and social expectations, the amplified family dynamics, the obsessive spurts and cluttered minds.

Looking for answers, we found that the majority of books on the market were too in-depth and lengthy for a busy engaged woman. They primarily focused on the planning realm, leaving us feeling even more overwhelmed. Already inundated by the logistical planning challenges ahead of us, we were put off by these cumbersome, detail-oriented books, and found them to be useless in addressing the nuances of our emotions.

As a result, we dreamed of putting together a different kind of book for brides, one that is emotionally supportive, informative and instructive, and whose learnings have utility and application after the wedding is all said and done. This book is inspired by the experiences of our clients and friends, and draws on interviews with brides and our own personal experiences.

Unveiling Weddings combines wedding narratives with comforting psychological advice.

It offers inspirational and engaging stories that normalize the emotional hurdles and pressures facing the modern bride. It integrates Western psychological strategies and Eastern concepts of mindfulness.

Unveiling Weddings will give you the emotional support you need to find clarity, balance, and pleasure in your life as the wedding day approaches. It will offer brides (and those who care) new insights into the wedding process so that as a culture we can challenge the myth of the inevitable blissful engagement. With an understanding of the emotional intricacies involved in being engaged, we can begin to encourage brides to show their genuine feelings—a welcome invitation to those brides who feel flabbergasted by their mixed emotions—and recognize the nuanced significance of this rite of passage.

It is our belief that the more a bride can laugh and stay in touch with her emotions before the "big" day, the better prepared she will be to handle the challenges along the way.

Unveiling Weddings is for a woman who wants to remember her wedding experience feeling empowered rather than traumatized, who wants to use this time as an opportunity to improve her relationship with herself, her fiancé, and the people around her. It is for brides who want to manage their emotional world, learn to respond instead of react, and who ultimately and optimally want to be nourished throughout the process.

We want this book to be the antidote to the madness of the wedding process. We hope that you find the content informative and engaging without being overwhelming. The goal is for you to feel supported by the stories and empowered by the wellness strategies.

Please note:

Both of our voices are incorporated within these pages. In order to simplify our writing, the pronoun "we" is utilized to convey a mutually agreed-upon experience or concept.

The stories within these pages are composites and combinations of stories from women with whom we have spoken and worked over the years. Some are great myths and legends passed down from one generation of brides to the next. As such, a few of the stories have been embellished to prove a point and to protect the brides who shared them when we felt some information was too personal to be published in a book. Permission was granted where needed and all the names have been changed. We would love for this book to keep growing. Please send us your stories and let us hear your own experience.

Read *Unveiling Weddings* in any way you choose. You can read front to back or you can flip through it to the chapters that interest you. Enjoy!

INTRODUCTION

Getting married is a rite of passage that for most brides provokes soul-searching and change. It is a transitional and transformative time. It is a time of decisions and examination. It is a time of excitement and joy, with a new beginning looming on the horizon. It may also be a time of shock and uncertainty, anxiety and obsessiveness. It can be a mixed bag of emotions, with brides finding themselves happy one minute and desperately sad the next.

One thing is for certain though—no matter how smart, how well-educated, how mature, how independent, how overjoyed, or how old you are, no bride is immune from these emotional twists and turns. Fortunately these highs and lows are not a sign that something is wrong. Instead, they are a sign that something is right. You are facing a significant life-changing event— you are getting married! And the fact that you may find this time to be challenging shows that your body, mind, and heart are paying attention. Just like how any other major life transition is personally and spiritually revealing, so too is the wedding process. It may be cliché, but it deserves restating to import the significance—getting married is a major rite of passage, and it needs to be treated and massaged as such.

Many high-functioning, confident brides have walked into our offices hesitant to admit that they are feeling "off," "stuck," "emotional," "neurotic" or "crazed." We hear them saying, "I know I am overreacting. It is only a wedding." But based on our clinical experiences, we can assure you that there is a 99% chance you are not overreacting. And on a relational level, think of every bride you have known in the past ten years; isn't it safe to say that the majority of them had struggles in that supposedly euphoric period between engaged and wed? Let's face it—modern brides are saddled with a ton of pressure to "perform," too much complexity in the multitude of decisions that need to be made, and oftentimes messy relationship noise that can complicate even our best efforts at maintaining sanity in the face of chatter.

Particularly aggravating is how our culture pressures brides to maintain a happy demeanor even though it might not feel authentic. Even though most rites of passage are inherently challenging—coming of age, launching from the nest, transitioning to the work force—our culture tends to not recognize the transition to marriage as an arguably trying one. We discourage brides from expressing or even feeling these upsetting emotions; after all, this is *supposed to be a happy time.*

Unfortunately, the dated tradition of expecting women to smile regardless of the situation still rings true with our brides. We want a bride to feign optimism, even though she is fighting with her mother, laugh despite having cold feet, beam with happiness while she is spending beyond her budget, and grin as she desperately tries to obtain an ultra-skinny wedding weight. And god forbid, if a bride dares to show any negative emotions, she puts herself at risk of being called "Bridezilla" by those who are supposed to love her the most.

However, the reality is not that our family and friends are uncaring and cold, but rather that there is a general lack of awareness about the emotional challenges that brides experience. The road from engaged to wed is fraught with challenges that far transcend the stereotypical planning concerns. Instead, this journey

compels each woman to take a hard look at her relationships, her values, and her identity in the face of being a
bride.

Chapter One

I Am Engaged,
But I Feel a Bit Zany

CHAPTER CONTENTS:

Emotional Myths

The Actual Reality: An Emotional Rollercoaster

The Actual Reality: An Emotional Tug-of-War

EMOTIONAL MYTHS

You are engaged. You are a fiancée. You are soon to be a wife. *Wow... Is this really my life?*

Each of these labels may feel like powerful new identifiers for you. These may be roles you have been anticipating your entire life or roles you never thought you would find yourself filling in a million years. Either way, the fact that you are now engaged may leave you feeling a bit dazed and confused. Confounding it all is the fact that you feel like you *should be* happy, euphoric, love-crazed, excited, and every other positive emotion under the sun. After all, you are ENGAGED.

But maybe you don't feel this way. Instead, you may be feeling a little anxious. You may feel alone in all the decisions ahead of you or smothered by too many cooks in the kitchen. Plenty of people are telling you what you should be jazzed about, but you are having a hard time feeling authentically excited. You may also have begun to fully understand the pressure that's ahead of you in planning a wedding—only aggravated of course by the picture-perfect ideals that you see in every bridal magazine, ideals that you are unsure you even want to replicate. The reality is starting to set—being engaged is not everything you thought it was going to be. You may even possibly dread some of it.

And worst of all, you may feel too afraid to admit your discomfort to anyone, because after all, *you should be happy*!

Myth: You <u>Should</u> Be Elated!

Therese and Greg had an epic engagement, one that would put even a reality tv show to shame. Riding the high of their emotional connectedness, Therese and Greg decided they wanted do something very *un*-wedding-like, elope in Las Vegas, and avoid the inevitable stress of any intricate planning (beyond hunting down a fabulous vintage Elivis-style suit for Greg).

Over the years, Therese had experienced the ups and downs of her friends' engagements, and these less-than-stellar sideline events informed her certainty that she wanted no part in a traditional wedding with "all that fuss." Compounding this, both Therese's and Greg's parents were no long alive, and it seemed logical that their friends would understand an elopement and the decision to spend their savings on a new condo instead. Plus, Therese and Greg planned to throw a low-key wedding bash at home after tying the knot in Vegas.

Although Therese felt relatively set about the plan to elope, after a few weeks she found herself feeling torn and unsure, questioning what had felt so certain just a month before. The more she got familiar with what it meant to be engaged, the more outside chatter clouded her mind. "I *should* have a traditional wedding. That's what getting married is about, right? Maybe Vegas is a terrible idea. And, *shouldn't* I be excited to plan what *should* be the happiest day of my life? Plus, my friends honored our friendship by making me part of their weddings. I *should* do the same in return."

The familial expectations reared their head as well. Therese's sister questioned the plan. "If you really feel the need to elope, shouldn't you do it in a classier place like the Caribbean?" Her aunt even had the audacity to announce, "Maybe this Greg guy isn't for you? If he was, you *would* be excited to plan a wedding."

In the end, Therese was able to let these doubts, questions, and *shoulds* go and get back in touch with what she really *wanted*. The Vegas elopement was as special and memorable as she envisioned, and Therese even managed to do some wedding planning that mattered to her. She created a Marilyn Monroe costume to complement her groom's Elvis outfit. They exchanged vows with cocktails in hand, and have never looked back.

The story of Therese and Greg illustrates the ultimate challenge of a bride—discerning between the *shoulds* of society and the *wants* of ourselves. This internal battle presents itself in our daily lives as well when we get trapped by the idea that we are *should* feel a certain way based on a particular situation. *You should be angry at Sally for flaking on you*; you *should be happy about your promotion*; you *should be excited about the upcoming camping trip.* Yet, you may not feel how others expect you to feel or what protocol dictates. You might be just fine with Sally. A promotion may provoke more anxiety than happiness. You may be dreading this adventurous excursion into nature. These societal expectations of the way you are supposed to feel are emotional myths.

The emotional myths of what it means to be a bride in our culture are enormous. You can probably call to mind a ton, but these probably sound most familiar:

- *You should feel blessed that you got engaged.*
- *You should want a wedding.*
- *You shouldn't have any uncertainty about your fiancé.*
- *Your wedding should be all-consuming and the most important aspect of your life right now.*
- *You shouldn't feel stress, as this is the happiest time of your life.*

And on and on and on...

However, you may not even recognize these as myths—and definitely through no fault of your own. Women have been indoctrinated by these notions, which have been propagated by the wedding industry and adopted as the collective should. But the reality is that most brides do not have these feelings. And that is why these ideas are fables, myths, half-truths, and likely not your personal reality.

The truth is that only you know how you feel. No one else is inside of your body and mind to interpret what is going on in there. We all have different histories, experiences, and emotional triggers that provoke different feelings, and that is why getting married is not a one-size-fits-all process.

THE ACTUAL REALITY: AN EMOTIONAL ROLLERCOASTER

Now that we have started the process of debunking how you should be feeling, let's tackle how you *are* feeling now that you are engaged.

You may say ... "where do I even start in explaining the complexities of how I feel?" Most commonly, brides feel as if they are on an emotional rollercoaster, with their emotions up, down, and all around. One day feels calm and content, the next feels anxiety-ridden and stressful. It's enough to make a bride question her sanity and wonder whether she is becoming that bride she has always detested.

It is understandable to feel frustrated when your emotions are more intense than normal. No one likes to feel emotionally overwhelmed, but that is what often happens in the midst of major life transitions. After all, a transition connotes newness, which may bring new feelings. Plus, transitions begin with an end, an end that may need to be mourned. In your case, with marriage on the horizon, you are ending your life as a single woman and all that this entails. It is a loss, and even though you are arguably excited about the gain, it is a loss nonetheless. Thus, an array of emotions is not a sign that something is wrong. *It is a sign that something is right.*

After all, love is a big, fat, complicated emotion, and getting married is inherently an emotional experience. It is exciting, sometimes scary, oftentimes confusing. It is at the very least a kiddie rollercoaster if not an upside-down one. Plus, it's not as if you can just snap your fingers and get married. You have to figure out *how* to get married. It's a lot to take in, not only on a philosophical level but also a logistical one.

"This Is Normal, This Is Natural."

You may shed a single tear or clean out a tissue box in one flood-filled session. You may raise your voice to levels that you didn't know existed within you. You may even carry a general level of nervousness throughout your entire engagement. However, at some point, you will want to surrender to the emotional rollercoaster rather than fight it.

So when you feel confused or panicked about what venue or dress to pick, repeat this mantra: *this is normal, this is natural.* You are getting married. You will *feel* and you will *feel intensely.* And nine times out of ten, you will have a very valid reason for your sentiments. You feel for a reason. So give yourself a break and remember, *this is normal, this is natural.*

✿ ✿ ✿

Annette and Sheila were yoga buddies. They have been going to the same Sunday morning yoga class for years. Although they never saw each other beyond the rubber mats, they enjoyed coming to class early and swapping tidbits about their lives. Coincidentally, they both got engaged around the same time. One Sunday morning at class, Annette confessed a dream she had been having at least once a week since becoming engaged. It was about her high school boyfriend, her first love, the man with whom she was first intimate. Annette could never remember any specific details about the dream, but it was most definitely of her high-school boyfriend, cementing himself as "the one" she always thought of when thinking about significant ex-boyfriends. Sheila, upon hearing Annette's ex-boyfriend dream let out a big, "ME TOO! AND I can't stop dreaming of an old fling I had when I lived abroad."

Laughing at these unexplained and unstoppable ex-boyfriend dreams was a relief for them in some ways. It was sign that their unconscious selves were normal. If they both had been dreaming of their exes, then this must be something that many women experience. At a deep intellectual and emotional level, Annette and Sheila were happily engaged and knew they had ended up with the right partners.

Being engaged is truly a time of transformation. It is a rite of passage that allows us to stand still and reflect on the past while also moving forward and planning for the future. Annette and Sheila remind us: it's okay to dream.

✪ ✪ ✪

THE ACTUAL REALITY: AN EMOTIONAL TUG-OF-WAR

Your loved one pulls your hand to the right. Almost concurrently, your mother pulls you to the left. Subsequently, your sister tugs you backwards, while at the same time a friend signals you straight ahead. As an engaged woman and soon-to-be bride, this scenario may not sound familiar in the literal sense but certainly may ring a few bells in the figurative sense.

This feeling of being pulled in multiple directions is common and complicated by the fact that you want to please the people you care about, yet you want to pursue your own course. After all, it is *your* wedding.

But as the following stories indicate, it is not always that easy to follow your own course. Relationships are dynamically charged, and even though you can rally around the *idea* of doing exactly what you want, it is very hard to do that.

✿ ✿ ✿

Andrea, a bride at 28 years-old, chose to include six bridesmaids from various areas of her life. While each was a kind, gentle soul when left to her own devices, with the fever of a wedding, each became a bit consumed, positioning for a dress in a shade and style that suited her own particular body type and coloring. Andrea's maid-of-honor spent hours picking out a few dress options, and Andrea felt strong-armed into picking the teal green strapless that her maid-of-honor liked the most. However, Andrea also knew that the teal green strapless was going to make her pale sister look sickly. Moreover, the color her maid-of-honor adored was one that Andrea's mother said she could not stand. Andrea felt pulled in multiple directions, unable to please everyone, feeling terribly guilty that she couldn't possibly make everyone happy.

✿ ✿ ✿

As soon as Stephanie got engaged, she began

to worry about who would walk her down the aisle. Her biological father was still alive, feigned some interest in her life, but was never really around. Her stepfather, on the other hand, had changed her diapers, taught her how to throw a football, and even helped her pick the DJ for the wedding. Stephanie was also fortunate enough to have an older brother who had also always been there for her and had indicated many times over the years that he would love to walk her down the aisle. Stephanie did not know what direction to take, and most importantly, she did not want to hurt anyone's feelings. She wished someone would just tell her what to do

Given the complexities, yet normalcy, of the situations that Andrea and Stephanie found themselves in, it is obvious that being engaged is an emotional rollercoaster. The notion of optimal bliss is a fable. Although elation during every second of your engagement would be fantastic, it is simply not a realistic expectation. Regardless, being engaged is one of those amazing once-in-a lifetime moments that we hope you end up cherishing despite the emotional twists and turns.

Becoming a Bridal Buddha
&
Beating the Beast of Bridezilla

———

CHAPTER CONTENTS:

Strategies for Becoming a Bridal Buddha

Reframing & Transforming Fear
Radical Acceptance
Just Relax
Behavioral Distractions
Emotional Distractions
Physical Distractions

Strategies for Beating the Beast-of-Bridezilla

How to Respond, Not React
Beware the Wedding Triggers
Making Room for Self

———

Now that the myth that you should be elated has been debunked, you may be feeling a bit better about your emotional ups and downs. *What do I actually do with them*??!

Emotional states obviously come and go throughout the day. Even as powerful and intense as they may feel in the moment, these feelings—anger, fear, sadness, disgust, surprise, curiosity, acceptance, and joy—are not permanent. Rather, they ebb and they flow.

In fact, the latest brain research suggests that an actual emotion lasts only 8 to 10 seconds. But, if this is true, why does it seem that your feelings of anger towards your in-laws persist for hours, days, or even weeks? Why does it appear that your anxiety is not only persistent but continues to grow as your wedding day draws nearer? The answer lies in what we *do* with that emotion and whether we allow it to linger.

STRATEGIES FOR BECOMING A BRIDAL BUDDHA

When you feel stuck and entangled by strong emotions, it is time to become a Bridal Buddha. We aren't asking you to go too hippie-dippy here, but we employ the symbolism of Buddha to connote calm, wise, detached reflection. Buddhas are adept at defusing and transforming emotions into a centered and calm state. They recognize that you are separate from your emotions, and that your emotions are fluid and transitory.

The visual of a river is particularly symbolic for the process of detachment. Emotions stream by, but they ultimately pass. You may be tempted to reach into that river and hold onto that feeling, harbor that resentment, feel pissed off just a bit longer, but you need to let that emotion stay in the river and pass.

✧ ✧ ✧

Patricia's wedding was to be a deliberately intimate event, as she had chosen to only invite close family and friends. And due to the size of the venue, it had been a struggle to cut down the list; subsequently her single friends did not have the option to bring a guest. A couple of weeks before the wedding, one of Patricia's closest friends called to say that her husband could not make the festivities. Since she didn't want to travel alone, she was going to bring a girlfriend in his place. Instead of asking permission, Patricia's (supposedly close) friend was adamant about this change and indicated she wouldn't be able to make the wedding if bringing a different date was an issue.

Needless to say, this conversation had Patricia reeling. It was simply not her friend's place to invite someone else. For god's sake, Patricia wasn't even letting her sister bring a date.

Despite a deep level of irritation, Patricia was able to employ her Bridal Buddha, calmly detaching from what could arguably leave her pissed for months. She went for a run, calmed herself down, and talked to her fiancé about the "rules" they set for the wedding and how they should approach this sticky situation. Once Patricia's calm yet concerned sentiments were shared with her friend, the friend rightly backed down, understanding the predicament in which she had placed her. Then, best of all, Patricia seemed to just move on to the next thing. She did not gossip about the drama or dwell on it. Rather she just let her anger be in the moment, then let it float down the river.

✿ ✿ ✿

From the first glance at a wedding magazine to the last dress fitting, Jane was barraged by her mother's passive-aggressive suggestions of how to make her wedding better. It was an endless litany of undermining advice. But by the time she was ready to walk down the aisle, Jane had found her Bridal Buddha.

Jane's mom: "You absolutely need to be in a limo or at least something classy—not Devon's old Mustang! It is the one-day of your life to splurge and to be classy for once. Plus, I think we should get a limo to take the whole family from the church to the reception. Everybody is going to be watching, and it is just proper thing to do." And then, giving in, but with an obvious roll of her eyes, she continues, "I guess it is your wedding and you can do what you want... but what are my friends going to think?"

Jane's Bridal Buddha: Jane listened but was detached from her mom's incendiary comments. She understood that these were her mother's emotions. *A bridal Buddha lets her mother's limo chatter float down the river!*

The stories of Patricia and Jane highlight how easily it could be to get consumed by the emotions of your wedding challenges. But they also highlight how conceptually easy it is to detach from them once you have made the decision to do so. You will find tremendous comfort when you remember that *you are not your emotions and that you have the power to choose to let them go.* Your emotions, no matter how intense or awful, will inevitably pass, particularly when you allow the role of Bridal Buddha to inform your role as Bride.

Bridal Buddha Strategy #1:
Reframing & Transforming Fear

Naturally, the thought of planning a wedding (details, details, details—ugh!), and getting married (committing to someone for eternity—yikes!), may make you feel a little apprehensive. It is a big deal, probably your biggest decision in life to-date. So of course you are scared and anxious. You are about to do a very brave thing, showing your love and commitment to your partner in front of all of your friends and family. You may feel out of your comfort zone, and your body, heart and mind are paying attention.

Many people interpret this type of fear as a bad thing. We want you to reframe it as a good thing. *Good things can indeed happen when you are nervous.* After all, haven't good things happened in your life when you have challenged yourself, pushed your edges, and embraced change? Those butterflies in your stomach reflect the excitement and anticipation of all the newness that is ahead of you.

Your challenge is to consciously reframe your thinking when anxiety and fear pop up.

Old interpretation: "Butterflies are bad news. If I am feeling anxious, something must be wrong."

New interpretation: "Butterflies are normal. I am just excited."

The Bridal Buddha acts from a place of thinking rather than feeling. She is able to detach from the emotion of it and instead rationally reinterpret that emotion. The Bridal Buddha doesn't have to be trained to mitigate her fear, she simply has to make that choice.

On the other hand, please do not ignore fear and anxiety that interferes with your functioning at home or at work. There is a distinct difference between healthy fear and neurotic fear. Debilitating fear or anxiety show that your intuition may be telling you something. Often these feelings are difficult for family members and friends to understand. If you feel that these fears need to be explored rather than reframed, schedule some time with your religious leader or a psychotherapist.

Bridal Buddha Strategy #2:
Radical Acceptance

Radical acceptance is an opportunity to dramatically shift your perception of yourself and the circumstances around you. Dr. Tara Brach is a clinical psychologist, author, and teacher of Buddhist mindfulness who developed this concept in her book called *Radical Acceptance*. She postulates that we are too hard on ourselves.

This fear of falling short may be amplified when you are a bride. The pressure to look and feel great is ever-present. You may find yourself trying to identify with the flawless bride who has done everything "just right"—from the shower to the cake to the vows. Striving for perfection is a natural way to protect yourself from your fears of not being enough, but in the end it further disconnects you from what is going on inside.

Radical acceptance is emotional freedom from your feelings of self-doubt. It is saying, "*I accept and I surrender to the process.*" When you accept your con-

cerns, you are no longer stuck stressing about everything that is not right, either internally or externally. In
fact, nothing is right or wrong. It just is the way it is. If
you fully accept that the wedding process is rife with
challenges, you are accepting your concerns as real, but
you are no longer succumbing to them. It is empowering to say *"yes, I can handle this"* to every emotion and
situation, no matter how difficult.

This is not to say that you will feel completely calm
and peaceful when one of your bridesmaids decides to
wear a boa with her dress. Sure, you may be upset, but
then what? *Yes, I am angry. Yes, I am fearful that my
wedding party will look idiotic. Yes, I am so sick of dealing with these details. But yet, this is okay. In fact, it is all
okay. This is just another detail with which I must deal.
There has got to be a way to make this work. What are
my options?*

And be mindful of the fact that it is not the initial
situation that is exhausting. It is the process of getting
stuck ruminating and stressing about the bridesmaid's
dress that is wearing you down. A negative emotion
only has power if we get trapped and entangled by it. If
you stuff it, mask it, push it back, or attach to it, you get
wrapped up in your reaction. It will haunt you for days
and grow bigger. One worry brings on another disappointment, and five minutes later you are in the pool of
negativity. If you accept the feeling and the situation for
only what it is in that moment, it will transform.

In the face of a distressing situation, it is important
to note that radical acceptance is not passive approval
or apathy. Radical acceptance is actively experiencing
your current emotional state without attempting to stop

or control it. In turn, you are developing your ability to step back and observe a situation, which allows you to find alternative solutions. No longer are you fixated on the problem. When you radically accept the situation, you are then free to seek a solution and move through it.

✿   ✿   ✿

Sally found out she was pregnant two months before her wedding. She and her fiancé were thrilled with the news, but they decided to not announce the pregnancy so close to the wedding. They did not want it to distract from the wedding and they thought it smart to keep the news private in case Sally had a miscarriage.

Yet, Sally started to worry about how she was going to have a bachelorette party without anyone being suspicious of her not drinking. As one normally not shy to throw back her chardonnay, it was going to be painstakingly obvious. Something that felt so sacred and special suddenly felt very stressful. While Sally still felt thrilled to be pregnant, she was also stressed and confused. She had always imagined a crazy night out on the town with her best friends, and now there was no way she could pull it off. And, compounding the dichotomy of joy and stress was a certain level of frustration. Why were all of these great things happening at once?

However, rather than mentally waging a battle with the situation, Sally decided to accept it, surrender to it and all of her mixed feelings, and to trust that everything would work itself out. She let go of the problem and gave it some time. Once she had accepted the reality, a solution easily presented it-self—spa service instead of bottle service! *Let go of the problem and receive the answer.*

✧ ✧ ✧

Bridal Buddha Strategy #3: Just Relax

Just relax. That's what everyone keeps telling you. *Relax, it's a wedding and it's supposed to be fun.* These well-intended "sage" bits of advice are a bit too general to do you any good. What you are really hearing is "*calm down, you crazy woman,*" when what you need to know is "*how the heck do I relax??*"

To become the optimal Bridal Buddha, you need an arsenal of relaxation tools in your back pocket. These can range from meditative, body-calming exercises to mental tricks, to pure behavioral changes. What's common about all of them is that they effectively *distract* you from what you are feeling, perhaps temporarily or perhaps permanently.

Some of the concepts below were originally developed by Marcia Linehan, Ph.D., who pioneered a new therapy called Dialectical Behavior Therapy that incorporates mindfulness techniques.

Distraction Attraction

Distractions are best used during crises to help reduce the impact of emotional events. While you may not consider your wedding to be a crisis per-se, the emotional turmoil might feel like a crisis.

Some people balk at a distraction strategy, as it appears to be simple avoidance. But, who says we should feel everything to the fullest all the time? We use hot pads to protect us from the stove, most women get an epidural for childbirth, and we rely on friends to avoid catastrophizing the smallest of mishaps. It is only normal, and in fact adaptive and necessary, to want to decrease your discomfort with the stress, the anxiety, or any other uncomfortable emotion—particularly transitory emotions of a wedding planning process.

So, to all you skeptics out there, a little distraction is actually very healthy and an excellent coping mechanism to get you through this challenging yet transitory time. As long as you are not engaging in excessive avoidance or using alcohol or drugs as your tool, give yourself a break and allow yourself to divert your attention away from the all-consuming wedding.

Behavioral Distractions

Non-wedding focused activities: You may have heard the mantra, *if you want to change one behavior, you have to replace it with another.* Enough said. If you find yourself spending an inordinate amount of time researching every possible floral combination and it's starting to drive you batty, it may be time to replace that behavior with another.

Rather than spending all your time trolling wedding websites, perhaps you need to refocus on your job. Rather than waiting by the phone for different vendors to call you back, perhaps it's time to reinstate the morning run. Rather than devoting every Saturday to planning, perhaps each Saturday needs to also involve a trashy novel or magazine while lounging on the sofa. Redirecting your energy to a different activity makes it impossible for that original behavior to take up so much space. And by taking yourself away from an all-consuming behavior and adopting a new one, you can come back to the task feeling renewed and with more focused energy.

Make it about someone else: Perhaps you are starting to notice that lately everything seems to be about you. Every conversation with your friends revolves around your wedding, most outings with your mother are about planning, and you realize you have lost track of what's going on in other people's lives. Now may be the time to take yourself outside of you and refocus your attention on someone else.

You may be engaging in a pity-party that your dress isn't going to be ready until a week before the wedding, but with a little effort, you likely can find someone else's problems for your energy. Go support your friend before she goes out on a blind date, talk your sister through her pre-interview anxiety, sit down and really ask your fiancé how he is doing. Focusing on others can give you a window to take a breather, gain some distance from your problems, all while making you feel good about yourself. After all, when all of this is over, you won't be a bride, but you will always be a friend, a sister, and a partner.

Mental Distractions

Shift worldview to improve your view: If you are like most brides, you waver between feeling justified in your stress and then shame for feeling so stressed. This latter sentiment is likely grounded in the realization that in the grand scheme of things your problems are good problems to have. By broadening your worldview and stepping back to refocus your attention on what other people are struggling with, you can regain perspective on our own situation.

Not to be too Mother Teresa, but if you are feeling like a charity case over how expensive the wedding is and wishing you had more to spend, perhaps it would help to reflect on how much you have in comparison to African children suffering from malaria or the migrant women who toil in the fields for pitiful wages. Or even just think about those people working for minimum wage who likely can afford only a fraction of the wedding you are having. You are blessed and fortunate to be in your situation. That's not to say you should feel guilty about it, but certainly try to keep your perspective and stay grounded.

Mentally go on your honeymoon: Ahhh... where will that yummy honeymoon place be? A beach bungalo in Thailand, an African safari, a tiki hut in Tahiti. Okay, perhaps those are a bit extravagant. But what about making one of these fantasy spots your mental honeymoon locale? Often our minds can be the best way to distract ourselves, and visualizing your personal "happy place," reflecting on a peaceful moment or dreaming of the future can be the best escape. Use your mind and imagination as a distraction, and see how far it can take you away from your present state of mind.

Physical Distractions

Our minds and bodies are connected, and when we offer our body new sensations, we can calm our mind. Think how helpful it is to take a hot shower, hold ice on a warm day, get a massage, and rub your hands and face with a hot towel on a stuffy airplane. These physical sensations give you emotional relief, and during this wedding time, they may feel like your most powerful tools to calm yourself.

TLC—Self-Soothing: We often do not give ourselves permission to nurture and pamper ourselves. Well, the rules have been reset and you are invited to do this—not only because it is your wedding but also because it reflects self-care. Even though you may not inherently relish the fancy clothes or the latest cutting-edge beauty treatment, these wedding perks tend not only to your physical wellbeing but also to your emotional wellbeing. And the permission to soothe and nurture yourself can be a lifelong valuable asset.

That's not to say your TLC needs to be superficial; the answer is very individual. If you have managed to soothe yourself in the past, think back and try to remember how you did it. Perhaps it was something really simple, like a hot bath.

To simplify even further, employ your five senses—those valuable tools of smell, taste, touch, hearing, and sight that you have relied on for soothing since your infancy. This could mean smelling the cologne on your fiancé's shirt, massaging your feet with hot oil, singing show tunes to yourself, looking at a sentimental photo, or throwing your chef's hat on for a little culinary therapy.

With your senses as an arsenal of soothing tools, think how accessible relief is. Imagine you are driving to an engagement party, feeling exceptionally nervous about two worlds of friends about to meet. You can't freak out to your fiancé, since he is meeting you there and you cannot reach anyone via cell phone. You are alone and starting to feel worse as time goes on. But wait! You are not alone. Your senses are with you and they can work to alleviate some of your anxiety. You take a few minutes in your car to rub your hands and stare at your engagement ring; it's a time-out moment using your senses of touch and vision, a break that tends to your tension and puts you in a different frame of mind.

Breathing Exercises: Try this scenario on: You have painstakingly gone over your invite list for weeks, running every single attendance scenario in your Excel spreadsheet, confident that no matter how you slice or dice it, there is no way that you will exceed your venue's maximum capacity of 150 guests. But the YES responses keep coming in, each envelope enveloping you in a bit more anxiety. And then it happens, 150, 151, 152... all the way up to 165. You are shocked, completely paralyzed and unable to appreciate the fact that so many loved ones actually want to come celebrate you. Instead, you feel like you may as well cancel the wedding; there is absolutely no way to exceed 150 guests. No solutions seem possible, no relief in sight.

Ok, breathe...

Now a deeper breath...

Some more belly breathing and a deep exhale...

Aha, you are already feeling better.

Breathing exercises can be one of the most powerful and effective tools to improve the tension of the moment. When we focus on our breath, we are changing both our body and mind. Breathing exercises can alter your heart rate, your nervous system, your circulation, all dramatically reducing your anxiety.

Remember this—it is physiologically impossible to feel anxiety while breathing deeply. These two states simply cannot co-exist.

For brides, breathing exercises are not only invaluable but also exceptionally versatile. They are yet another tool small enough to fit in your metaphorical purse, available to be pulled out whenever the need may arise. They can help you fall asleep and escape the nighttime planning worries; they can be your "medication" in reducing your anxiety about confronting your fiancé over his lackluster planning, and ultimately they can be your best friend as you calm your nerves before walking down the aisle.

✧ ✧ ✧

Tara's breathing exercises were a life saver throughout her engagement, but they were especially helpful right before she walked down the aisle. On the day of her wedding, there was a huge construction detour on the very road to her wedding location. After some savvy maneuvering by her limo driver, she was lucky to be at the church on time. Nevertheless, she was rattled and it was difficult to feel serene as she sat with her father in the car outside of the church.

As four o'clock struck, she could hear the wedding music playing inside, and she imagined her bridesmaids walking down the aisle. She started to visualize what it was like in the church, but this potentially momentous moment was jolted, as the nervously chatty driver started jabbering. Tara interrupted her driver and politely asked for silence, realizing she had been surrounded by noise all day. She paused to check in with herself. She noticed that her body was tense and there was a dull ache between her temples. She started taking deep slow breaths. The silence and the breathing felt great. Her dad noticed, and he too took a few deep breaths. Within minutes she could feel her body relax and her head stopped throbbing. A calm, centered feeling came over her. She stepped out of the car feeling relaxed and never looked back.

✿　✿　✿

There are a myriad of ways to engage in effective breathing, and below are a few to get you started. Find a breathing exercise that works for you, and feel free to modify and personalize it to maximize the benefits.

[Note: Please consult your doctor before attempting these exercises, especially if you have asthma, breathing problems, or health problems that adversely may affect you.]

✿　✿　✿

Breathing Exercise #1 —Basic Breathing

1. **Get into a Comfortable Position**
    This position would ideally have you lying flat on your back. However, if you do not have the luxury of doing this, get into a position that allows you

maximum lung capacity and circulation. Uncross your legs and arms and find a position that is comfortable. You can either close your eyes or keep them open.

2. **Take a Deep Breath**
   As slowly as you can, take a deep breath through your nose. Slowly fill up your lungs. Count to ten if that helps. Notice the air filling you up. Notice the air come into your body.

3. **Slowly Release**
   Slowly release your air through your mouth. Release it to a count to 10. Notice your body releasing the air.

4. **Slowly repeat steps 1-3 as many times as needed.**

Breathing Exercise #2—Quick Breathing

1. **Get into a Comfortable Position, as described above.**

2. **Take Quick But Deep Breaths.**
   Take one really quick yet deep, strong breath in through your nose.
   As you do this, try to keep your eyes very wide open.

3. **Exhale Naturally.**
   Let the air release naturally and slowly, relaxing your body and closing your eyes. Let your body relax.

4. **Repeat, each time letting your body feel even more relaxed.**

Breathing Exercise #3—Inner Child Breathing

1. Get a children's bubble bottle (or a brown paper bag).
2. Get into a comfortable position.
3. Take a deep breath in through your nose.
4. Slowly try to blow the biggest bubble you possibly can.
5. Keep slowly blowing big bubbles, each time relaxing different parts of your body.

STRATEGIES FOR BEATING THE BEAST OF BRIDEZILLA

Let's be honest. We all have an inner Bridezilla who could potentially come out under the right circumstances.

Unless you are a Buddhist monk, you surely can remember a time when you lost your cool and reacted strongly to something that didn't merit such a strong reaction. Perhaps you felt justified at the time but likely you felt embarrassed afterwards. Planning a wedding is rife with situations that can trigger such reactions.

Beating the Beast of Bridezilla Strategy #1: How To Respond, Not React

An emotional reaction is an *unfiltered* response that is triggered with little or no prior thought; it is detached from your intellectual filter. It's bursting into tears when a bridesmaid gives you her unsolicited opinion about the dress that you picked out for her. It's becoming furious when your fiancé asks to relax after work rather than diving into the endless planning details.

Just like your emotional rollercoaster, the tendency to react inappropriately is completely normal and natural, especially given the heightened sensitivities that accompany a wedding. However, it's time to empower you with the ability to *respond* instead of *react*.

An *emotional response* is possible when we take a minute to step back and evaluate an emotionally charged situation. If you allow for logic to be your filter, then inevitably a more reasoned response is possible. In essence, you are creating your emotional state rather than being run by it.

Let's differentiate between a reaction and a response.

Situation: Your fiancé is in charge of planning the honeymoon but hasn't even opened a web browser to start looking for flights, hotels, activities.

Bridezilla Reaction: You think about what a jerk he is and you conclude he must not care. You feel angry, disappointed, and hurt. You shout, *"You must not care at all about our honeymoon, not to mention me!"*

Bridal Buddha Response: You think about how much his inaction bothers you, but you remind yourself that his lack of initiative does not mean that he does not care. You feel mildly frustrated, but generally okay. You try not take things personally, and you trust that he will follow through because he is a good guy. After all, that is why you are marrying him. You take a deep breath and calmly say, *"When you have a moment, would you mind giving me me an idea when you will be ready to talk about our honeymoon? I am really looking forward to it and I would love to be able to picture where we are going."*

Notice how your anger can be diffused by responding rather than reacting. Additionally, the first reaction would likely only cause your fiancé to withdraw even more, and such an aggressive reaction clearly would not be motivating for him. Instead, the Bridal Buddha Response allows *him* room to respond rationally rather than react.

Situation: The block of rooms you have set aside for your guests expire in a week, and none of your guests have bothered to book them.

Bridezilla Reaction: You think that everyone so rudely refusing to book within the timeframe are ungrateful and lazy. In turn, you feel hurt and sorry for yourself. You "flame-mail" your guests, telling them to book or else suffer the consequences.

Bridal Buddha Response: You think about how busy your friends are and how easy it is for travel plans to get lost in the mix of life. You may still feel a little hurt, but deep down you know that your friends love you and want to celebrate your big day. Over dinner, you ask your fiancé about the idea of sending a friendly reminder email.

These examples are extreme. Yet, they illuminate how negative thoughts and interpretations of situations lead to reactive behavior as well as destructive feelings. Notice that in both of these examples, the end result of the wedding planning is the same—*a reminder email needs to be sent to your guests regarding who is attending*. However, the feelings and the direction to get there are radically different.

Beating the Beast of Bridezilla Strategy #2: Beware the Wedding Triggers.

To survive the chaos that you likely find yourself in, it's important to be aware of your emotional triggers. Essentially, *what is it in this crazy world of wedding planning that sets me off?* These triggers can be as subtle as your mom's facial expressions, any delay in friends or vendors getting back to you, or even something as ostensibly benign as the fact that your friends are offering to throw you a shower. You may find yourself in an emotional mess more frequently than you care to admit, and you are left wondering what it is that propels you to feel this way.

Taking an emotional inventory allows you to pinpoint what is triggering your reaction. Pretend you are a reporter investigating this mysterious situation that you call your emotional world. You need to dive in head first, ask a myriad of questions, all in an effort to understand what is *preceding* your feelings.

The following questions are key to identifying what states may trigger you into a tizzy.

- When exactly did I start feeling like this? What was going on for me that day?
- What is going on in my body? Was I tired or hungry?
- Who was there? Do certain people seem to be triggers for me?
- Where did this all occur? Is that place a particular spot of sensitivity for me?

Yvonne, not one to be overly emotional, burst into tears upon receiving a book from her friend Stacy, just a month before her wedding. The book, *The Art of Thank Yous,* was beautiful and thoughtful, but for some reason it made her feel exceptionally sad. At first, Yvonne wondered why she was so emotional about this arguably benign book. In doing an emotional inventory, it did not take long for Yvonne to see that there was a perfect storm of potential triggers for such a reaction: a sense of guilt that so many friends were giving so much (just as Stacy had in sending the book), a looming sadness that the wedding would soon be over (with the next step being thank you notes), and the internal insecurity that Yvonne carries with her each and everyday over her dyslexia (thus making her feel like the gift was very pointed). She was so grateful to have a thoughtful friend like Stacy, but the triggers had aligned for a visceral emotional reaction.

✿ ✿ ✿

While waiting for a table at their favorite brunch place, Vicki pulled out her phone to take a few pictures of her fiancé, Pete. As Vicki flipped through the pictures to show him the ones she had just taken, she accidentally showed him another picture on her phone—her wedding dress. And not just a picture of her dress, but one of Vicki actually wearing it. Pete looked at her with a blank expression. He was clearly disappointed, being the traditional type who romanticized that first glimpse of his bride walking down the aisle. *"How could you do that?",* Pete pointedly asked. Vicki felt the heat rising to her face and started to get teary. She repeated *"I'm so sorry, I'm so sorry."* Tears streamed down her face. Vicki felt as if all of her efforts to plan a magical wedding had been spoiled in one foolish bout of carelessness.

While this situation felt catastrophic at the time, by evening the couple recognized that they had over-reacted. Both had been tired, hungry, and stressed. They needed more sleep. They had been working late and spending every spare moment planning their wedding. Given their shaky mental and physical fortitude at the time, they were not equipped to handle the unexpected revelation of the dress. It was a lesson learned—there are physical triggers that can lead to unnecessary emotional reactions—and clearly such an overreaction was a cue that they were plain exhausted.

Not only is an emotional inventory useful for getting a grip on negative triggers, but it can also help you understand what breeds happiness for you. You can do the same exercise of "investigative reporting" in uncovering the external circumstances that bring you joy. Perhaps you always feel calm around a particular friend; maybe the artistic nature of making place cards is something that makes you feel fulfilled; or perhaps you have noticed that you tend to enjoy the wedding planning with your fiancé but not with your mom. This is rich, valuable data that you can use to structure your wedding planning process so that it feels a bit more pleasurable than strained, and a bit more meaningful than what you may have experienced to date.

Identifying trigger points allows you to be empowered by knowledge and avoid the Beast of Bridezilla.

Beating the Beast of Bridezilla Strategy #3: Making Room for Yourself

As you set forth in this journey of planning your wedding, you have received a personal invitation (perhaps engraved!) to honor your feelings and make room for yourself. This sounds simple, yet it is hard to put this principle into reality when you may be feeling pulled in so many directions.

We often think of space as literal, a physical carveout in a room, for example. However, during this engagement process, expand your thinking of space to be more figurative, encompassing your feelings, emotional energies, spiritual thoughts, as well as your big dreams, needs, and desires. If you have already moved in with your fiancé, you would not have let him take over the whole house with his stuff and baggage. However, we sometimes let people take over our emotional spaces and forget to validate our own feelings.

Amy and Eric sometimes wondered if they were actually even invited to their own wedding. Since both sides of their families were generously contributing, they felt compelled to invite many of their parents' friends and to hear (and sometimes adhere to) every little suggestion from their moms. Amy and Eric shouldered a sense of indebtedness to their families, making it particularly hard to push back and make room for themselves, even though rationally they knew they were the ones who should matter most.

The goal is to make enough room for yourself so that you feel prioritized in the wedding world of decisions. You need to make room for not only your wishes and dreams, but also for the so-called trivial things that matter to you. Asking for what is important—whether it be a particular china pattern or an extravagant floral arrangement—is an essential component to being a Bridal Buddha.

If you feel uncomfortable with your fiancé for having a stripper at his bachelor party, express your feelings. If you feel angry with your mom for not understanding your desire for a certain style of wedding dress, calmly express your thoughts. If you would prefer that your fiancé's ex-girlfriend not be invited to your wedding, speak up. If you want a religious ceremony, honor your values. Make room for you. Honor each feeling you have.

However, given the traditional role that has been engendered for women for centuries, we would be remiss to not mention that this process can be quite complicated. Women have been the primary caregivers for generations and have taken the more passive role within relationships. Even though our modern society has dramatically changed, we unconsciously expect women to be more flexible with their needs than is expected for their male counterparts. When a man firmly asks for a desire to be met, he feels entitled to ask for it. Yet, women oftentimes are missing this sense of entitlement to speak up, especially considering how society often belittles and barks at women who do as much.

Therefore, as you awaken your inner bridal maven, you may be hit with resistance for making room for yourself. This resistance may not only come from those around you but also from within yourself, a general insecurity around your sense of worthiness, particularly when it comes to the material nature of a wedding. It is hard to wrap your head around all that goes into a celebration of *you*.

You will be showered with gifts throughout your engagement and wedding, but one of the greatest gifts you can give to others (and to yourself) is to honor your real authentic self. Sometimes, we fail to express our needs because we want to avoid conflict; yet, avoiding conflict in the beginning can actually cause bigger conflicts in the end—resentments or anger may build. It is likely that people want to do things for you, want to hear you, want you to get dreams fulfilled. However, you need to feel secure within yourself to ask. This is your time to carve out space for yourself, break the traditional social norms, squash your own personal inertia, honor your feelings, and make a big festive space for YOU.

Chapter Three:
The Dreaded (or Perhaps Desirous) Process of Planning

CHAPTER CONTENTS:

**Choosing Your Planning Principle –
Enjoy the Adventure, Let It Be Easy**

What's Important to Me?

The Art of Compromise Without Giving Up Your Needs

**Decisions, Decisions —Beating out the Shoulds,
Musts, & Have-Tos**

Tricks of the Trade for Making Decisions

Obsession Confession

Creating a Stress-Free Wedding Zone

P lanning ... ahhhhh ... where does one even start in tackling this mountain of details, tasks, and endless decisions? Perhaps planning feels like a necessary evil, or maybe you have dreamed of this day since first grade. Either way, it is a big task and one that requires research. Fortunately for you, there are an immense number of books that can help you through the intricacies of planning, from venues to etiquette to menu choices. While this is not one of those books, it can help you with the internal research about what it means to be getting married.

While wedding planning is probably the single greatest trigger of bridal stress, we are more interested in helping you through the psychological aspects that inform your planning process. We won't teach you the tricks for creating affordable floral centerpieces, but we will teach you to manage all the choices. We don't know a thing about invitations, but we can help you identify your priorities, so you are clear on who you want to include in this special celebration. And while we may not offer any tips about creating your gift registry, we will leave you with the gift of knowing how to compromise.

CHOOSING YOUR "PLANNING PRINCIPLE" – ENJOY THE ADVENTURE, LET IT BE EASY

You do not have to be good.
You do not have to walk on your knees
for a hundred miles through the desert
repenting.
You only have to let the soft animal of your body
love what it loves.

Wild Geese—Mary Oliver

Enjoy the adventure. Let it be easy. What a beautifully succinct mantra to guide your wedding planning process. But easy does not necessarily mean simplicity. In fact, you can have the most intricate, extravagant wedding worthy of *Martha Stewart Weddings*, but you can *choose* to make the planning process enjoyable and easy. It's all in your attitude and in your ability to detach from the inherent stress of it, stay grounded in your principles and passions, and view it not as a hassle but as an adventure.

Let this be your launching pad for a new "planning mindset" ... *Enjoy the adventure. Let it be easy.*

Getting Started – What's Important to Me?

Molly had never given much thought to her wedding. She always assumed she would marry, but she never was one to dream about what it would actually look like. She had been to plenty of weddings herself, served as a bridesmaid countless times, but the details of a wedding had never interested her much.

Once engaged, Molly found herself feeling paralyzed by where to even start. She knew there were essential components to any wedding – invitations, music, dress, cake – but it was hard to tackle any of these details without knowing *what kind of wedding* she really wanted. Molly saw the merits of big, grand weddings (which meant including all of their family and friends) but was unsure whether it reflected her personality or her budget. She felt drawn to the idea of a spontaneous and intimate gathering but worried that she would regret not including so many of her loved ones. Another level of confusion arose around her fiancé's Catholicism, as church or religion had never been her thing. Molly simply had not reflected on what *was important to her,* so it was hard to know where to even start.

Molly's situation is quite familiar to many women, particularly those who are mentally starting from scratch. No internal planning had preceded Molly's engagement; so now she had to tackle the big picture of it all – concurrently researching not only the logistics but also her own internal values.

Even if you are a bride who has already created

your mental wedding database, *it is absolutely essential to take some time to name what is important to you for your wedding.*

Step 1: Figure Out Your Priorities

Ideally, this list should be more conceptual than tactical. Rather than prioritizing "no more than 50 people," record your priority as "an intimate gathering of close family and friends." Rather than specifying that you want a salsa band, make your priority a "high-energy, festive celebration." By being more general, you won't get too boxed in once the planning actively starts.

A sample priority list could include:

1. Create a wedding that both my fiancé and I are happy about.
2. Stay within a pre-determined budget.
3. Commence our union in a meaningful religious ceremony.
4. The more the merrier – include as many family and friends as possible.

After completing this list (perhaps over the course of a couple of days), circle the three most important priorities for your wedding. Post the list on a place where you can see it, and visit when need be. Keeping these big-picture conceptual priorities at your fingertips will not only keep you on track but will diffuse any stress or anger that gets triggered by the mundane (and the ridiculous!). Remind yourself of the *real reasons* you are getting married. It is most likely not about the cost of the band, but it is about the love for your fiancé and your desire to have your family and friends share in the celebration of it.

✿ ✿ ✿

Just a week before her wedding, Anika felt like she was going to to lose her mind. She had spent countless hours late at night cranking out the table placecards (in calligraphy of course) and then burning a personal CD for each of her guests. She had lost yet more weight, necessitating another dress alteration. Plus, she felt behind at work where she was trying to prepare her co-workers for her three-week wedding and honeymoon. In addition, her in-laws were arriving in a few days, and their apartment looked like it had been burgarlized by wild animals. She was having fun with some of the planning, yet the stress crept in as she wondered how she was possibly going to get everything done on time.

And then the final blow to her fragile demeanor hit. Anika and her fiancé had chosen to get married the weekend after Valentines Day, not realizing that it was an extremely popular date to get married. As such, with a week to go before the wedding, there was a shortage of flowers. When Anika confirmed the final number of boutonnieres, the florist casually told her the final cost. Somehow the original estimate had increased by $2,000!! How could adding three extra boutonnieres possibly do that? When she questioned the price, the florist said, "Oh, yeah it looks like my assistant quoted you incorrectly the first time; I am sorry, that is my final number." Anika was pissed. The florist refused to budge from her "new" price. Anika called several other florists to no avail, as it was the busiest flower day they had ever seen.

Anika felt stuck, a bit hopeless, and needless to say extremely angry at this florist. She did not want to give her a single cent, let alone more than she had budgeted. That night over dinner Anika and her fiancé revisited their priorities, returning to the list they had created months ago.

1. A beautiful and meaningful wedding celebration.
2. Stay within our budget.
3. Enjoy our engagement as much as possible.

With these priorities at the forefront of her mind, Anika started to figure out what to do. She realized that the flowers per se were not a necessity to create a "beautiful and meaningful wedding celebration." Recognizing this, Anika decided to have flowers only at the ceremony, ditch the flowers for the reception, and use candles instead. This fix kept them within their budget, meeting their second priority. And by staying on top of her first two priorities, the third priority was naturally fulfilled.

As for how to handle the nasty, unethical florist... Well, who wants to spend the week before her wedding arguing with a florist? She tabled the ensuing fight, deciding to potentially revisit it after the wedding, and instead enjoyed her "engagement as much as possible" in that special final week.

✿ ✿ ✿

Pinpointing the *core priorities* of your wedding is not only important for planning but it reinforces and reminds you of your identity and your values. By having your priorities clear, you can *enjoy the adventure* and *let it be easy.*

Step 2: Identify the Major Players

Ideally, your goal is to make you and your fiancé happy—not everyone else. However, you don't get married in a bubble, nor does the wedding get planned in one. While it is your choice on how to manage your family and friends, it is important to identify the key players—parents, siblings, grandparents, church officials—that you want to invite onboard.

That's not to say you want your mom to be your mini-me nor your sister's overly booked social schedule to dictate the wedding date, but at minimum you want to make sure they at least feel considered.

Be specific (at least within your mind) about whom you want the major players to be. Write them down, be concrete about it, as this will serve as your guide and filter for how to proceed with planning. While it will likely be almost impossible to adhere to your guidelines throughout the planning—after all, how can you say no to Great-Granny Shoo, who so thoughtfully wants to share her own wedding vows with you. At least you will have your own personal map to refer to when bumps appear in the road.

Step 3: Spread the Word

This may seem obvious, but once you decide what is most important to you, communicating your priorities is the next step. People cannot read your mind. If your mother keeps on recommending a church when you have your heart set on an outdoor wedding, you will tear your hair out. You are pre-empting the threat of looming battles if you take the time to spread the word. After all, the best defense is a good offense.

✿ ✿ ✿

In retrospect, Dakota wishes she had spread the word better during her engagement, especially to her parents. When Dakota was planning her wedding she felt like her parents were on their own mini honeymoon. They gave her a check and then basically left the rest to Dakota. Every once in a while her parents would call and passively criticize her choices about venue, flowers, the wedding date, whatever their little gripe of the moment seemed to be. "Oh dear! You decided on that caterer?"

For some people this hands-off approach might be a dream come true, but Dakota felt very alone planning her wedding, and she was unable to express her priorities. She so desired a small, outdoor wedding in her family's backyard. Instead she somehow was managing a wedding for her parents' friends at a fancy hotel downtown. Topping that, she did not feel that she had the right to communicate how stressed she was to her parents. Dakota even heard her mom brag about the situation at the rehearsal dinner. When asked if wedding planning had been difficult and time-consuming, her mom replied, "Oh, no. It has really been a piece of cake. She got the perfect location, with no drama, and not a whole lot of work."

Hearing this made Dakota's blood boil. Her mother had no clue how traumatic planning the wedding had been for her. However, she was mostly mad at herself for not spreading the word.

✿ ✿ ✿

As a bride, Dakota did not spread the word or ask for the help she needed. She ended up feeling alone and resentful. Communicating how demanding wedding planning had been and getting some help from her parents would have radically changed the wedding planning process for her.

The Art of Compromise Without Giving Up Your Needs

Planning a wedding requires you to take on a second job, albeit one that's unpaid and that takes up an inordinate amount of time, all with the hope that it will "pay" in the form of warm fuzzy memories.

And as with any work project, you have to interact with a cross-section of people, both familiar and unfamiliar, to complete this one big project. You have to be sensitive to the religious necessities of your priest while also taking into account your fiancé's atheism. You have to be respectful of your mom's desire to invite her entire book club, while also respecting the budget you have set for yourself. This huge undertaking requires finding a balance between openness to others and attention to self. It's finding that balance of *compromise* at the height of the chaos.

Weddings are obviously fraught with scenarios that call for compromise. This is fueled by the fact that a wedding spreads a firestorm of feelings among many significant people in your life—from your parents to your siblings to your friends. It feels like a big event not just for you but also for those who love you. That's why it is easy for some unsightly behavior to seep in. Your aunt may have a meltdown because her new boyfriend is not invited to the wedding. Your bridesmaid may have a fit because she does not look good in green. Your sister may find it hard to be excited for you because she herself is not coupled. The opinions, advice, and dilemmas (and sometimes selfishness) are endless.

You need to come prepared to this endure this firestorm of advice, *brace yourself* for the inevitability of it, and know you can deflect it. With knowledge that this storm is heading your way and the ability to compromise without losing yourself, you will more aptly prepare to protect yourself from it.

But, before we even get to the matter at hand, you may honestly ask... *But this is MY wedding, why do I need to compromise?* Well, the reason is very simple. A wedding is inherently a relational event, involving those other than yourself—at the forefront is your fiancé, and tailing behind are other important people in your life. It is a rite of passage that is ostensibly about you, but one that has also been informed by those around you. That's why other people matter—it's just the degree to which you let them matter and the degree to which you will allow for compromise.

Being In Your Own Boat

From the very beginning it is important to set sail and *practice being in your own boat*. This may feel self-indulgent, particularly since we have already recognized that a wedding is an interpersonal event, but this choice to sail your own boat is essential to your survival. Your boat will sink otherwise.

The art of compromise is about saying "No, I have my own thoughts and feelings," and "Yes, I can take your needs into consideration without feeling run over by them." By *being in your own boat,* you are taking the time to pause, separate from the situation, and assess your own needs. This mindset gives you a foundation to sail into the storm of opinions and provides a framework from which to compromise.

Let's take Malia, a bride who had never imagined wearing a veil at her wedding. This idea was something that Malia had loaded into her theoretical "boat." But as it turns out, Malia's mother was dead set on her daughter wearing a veil, not for any other reason than her heart being set on the idea. It was a subject that her mom continued to bring up delicately, initially aggravating Malia and rocking her boat a bit. But because Malia took the time to pause and assess the importance of her own needs, she ultimately realized that wearing a veil was something on which she could compromise and still *remain in her own boat.*

Consider another example, one that could hypothetically be torn from your wedding diary. Let's say you call your parents to finalize the details of the catering budget. Your dad answers the phone and you hear your mom yelling in the background. Instantly you know they have been fighting about the very thing you are calling about. How easy would it be to blame yourself for the fight? The very thought of them fighting could be enough to put you in a bad mood for the rest of the day. Or you may find yourself full of guilt because the wedding is costing so much money. You may even be tempted to mediate and get yourself mixed up in their drama. But at what cost?

Rather, you have the choice to stay the course and remain *in your own boat*. If you can pause, separate, and get in touch with your needs, you can then get off the phone without taking on any blame, getting involved in their conflict, or feeling any unnecessary guilt. Your parents are adults. The budget decision is a conflict between the two of them and not you. They need to deal with this issue (and other tough calls that they face) without your help. If there is a budget concern, they should sit down with you at a later date when all three of you can have a practical and rational discussion.

But *being in your own boat* may require not just a separation from the situation and an assessment of *your own needs*, but also a direct confrontation of the *other person's needs*. This becomes particularly necessary during what we will call "messy situations".

✿ ✿ ✿

The Rules of Fighting Fairly
- Face-to-face is better than texting. Try to have the most direct form of communication in order to really understand one another.
- Stay focused on the topic at hand. Don't bring up the past or another unresolved issue.
- It is okay to walk away ... for now. Yet, have an agreement that whoever closes the argument needs to initiate a renewed discussion within

the next 12-24 hours.

- Leave others out. Don't bring other people's thoughts and opinions into your discussion.

- Be kind and wise. Choose what you fight over and the words you use carefully. No one "wins" when insults are flying around.

- Listen, Listen & Listen—don't just prepare your argument.

- State your feelings clearly and explicitly. Do not assume your partner, friend or family member can read your mind or knows what is going on in your heart.

- Don't force others to be a clone of you. Allow other people to have different feelings and opinions.

- Honesty is the key to apologies. Don't jump to the post-fight kisses if you or your partner does not really mean it yet. Be honest with him/her and with yourself.

Here's a messy situation you can hopefully avoid. Let's pretend your groom and your mom start fighting about the music for your reception. In a moment of heightened emotion, your mom starts attacking your groom's taste in music, taking it even further to include insults about his friends. She threatens, *"Over my dead body will there be rap music at my daughter's wedding! I do not care what type of music appeals to your hoodlum friends."* After witnessing this irrational attack on your future husband, how easy would it be for you to just burst into tears or even get mixed up in the drama?

At this point, you might want to call a *time-out*. This heated situation needs to be diffused and perhaps discussed at a later time. This time-out can be as quick as a few moments or as long as a few days. But once you return to the "mess," your goal is to reach a compromise.

One option is to ask everyone, including yourself, to stop and take an internal inventory of thoughts, feelings, and expectations about the music at the wedding. Encourage your mom and fiancé to express their opinions of the situation, one at a time, with no interruptions or interjecting, and no attacking or defensiveness.

Once your mom hears that your groom is feeling concerned about whether his friends will feel comfortable and have a good time, she may feel more flexible and more able to compromise. In the end, it is likely your mom will agree that it is important that your fiancé's guests feel as comfortable as everyone else. When people are given the chance to better understand the context and emotions underlying one another's needs, there is a softening that allows for the art of compromise.

Once all the information is on the table, you will want to shift the focus from the problem (everyone has different musical tastes) to the solution (a string trio during appetizers and a DJ after the cake is cut). If your mom and fiancé gravitate back to arguing, gently remind them they are looking for a solution and not more problems. Another heated discussion can be avoided by saying something like: "I totally understand your concern, but right now we are looking at our options. Let's take some time to brainstorm other solutions."

As your wedding day approaches, whether you are

picking out your china, choosing the menu, or finalizing your guest list, you will encounter the need to make a compromise at every turn. It is too easy to get lost in the thoughts and feelings of family and friends. But by *practicing being in your own boat,* you will dramatically alter how you experience the wedding process—for the better! You will not be part of the drama, but part of the solution. You will demonstrate that you are not only "bride-in-chief" but also "friend/daughter/partner-in-chief."

DECISIONS, DECISIONS, DECISIONS—BEATING OUT THE "SHOULDS, MUSTS & HAVE-TO'S"

Celine was not born with a silver spoon in her mouth, but she grew up in a well-educated middle-class family. When it came to wedding planning, she felt uneducated about the appropriate wedding etiquette and ill-prepared to manage all of the vendors and family members. Like many brides, Celine felt this cultural pressure to suddenly know how to do things "properly." She was nervous about how the invitations should look/read, how to address certain people on place cards, who "should" be in the wedding party, who she "must" invite to her bridal shower, and how the ceremony "should" go. Celine often felt clueless about what she was doing, and all the wedding planning seemed to fall on her shoulders.

Although Celine's mother offered to help time and again, she never followed through. Celine asked her mom to come up with a list of invitees for her bridal shower, but weeks later there was still no list. Her mother, who is French, remarked, *"You know I have never been to an American wedding or a bridal shower. I am just not sure who should be invited."* Ugh! Her mom did not know either. She consulted the wedding magazines and the Internet, hoping they would be her knowledge-able friend on etiquette. But in the end, when it came to making decisions about her wedding, Celine felt lost in navigating the "shoulds, musts, and have-to's" and was pretty much on her own.

As Celine's scenario demonstrates, there is most definitely a protocol that society has reinforced when it comes to what a wedding *should* look like, *must* involve, and *has to* entail. *You should send save-the-dates. You must let your father walk you down the aisle. You have to have cake.* These and others are powerful messages and undeniably hard to escape. This paradigm makes it particularly difficult for a bride to find room or courage to apply her own *wants.*

In making the endless decisions that weddings in-volve—from color schemes to save-the-dates to regis-tries—you are constantly being called upon to decide what you want. But it's challenging to decipher what you really *want* from what you think you *should* do.

The good news is that the way we *perceive* these things can change everything. It may be really hard to clear the brush and realize there is another way to see it or do it, but by changing the lens through which you see your wedding, it loosens the rigidity of the *shoulds* and allows rooms for the *wants.*

Tricks of the Trade for Making Decisions

Decisions Trick #1 – Making Room for Multiple Choice Answers.

An effective way to kick out those mandates is to force yourself to come up with different options for situations that feel like absolutes. You might feel that you *have* to go over-budget for your dress, that your invitations *should* be timeless, and that you *must* invite your "frienemy" Bethany.

However, what other possibilities could you come up with beyond these single answers? Pull out the old paper and pen, and mentally create an old school multiple-choice question to address the lingering indecision.

For example, do I invite Bethany to my wedding?

a. I must invite Bethany to the wedding! Even though we have had our challenges, she is a good old friend.
b. If I can budget Bethany into the wedding, that would be great.
c. Bethany will understand if I do not invite her. She gets the complexities of weddings and how hard guests lists are.

Similar to how eye doctors provide you with multiple choices for which lenses work better … "better one, better two…" you need to try on different lenses and see which option is optimal for you.

Creating multiple-choice questions helps you expand beyond black and white thinking, put an end to societal absolutes, get you unstuck from indecision, and unveil other possibilities that likely better address your wants.

Decision Trick #2—Locate Your Intuition.

Often when you listen to your gut, you discover you have the answers within yourself. You can probably recall a moment in your life when you just followed what you knew was true without hesitation. You were letting your intuition lead the way without second guessing yourself. Life flowed simply, fell into place easily, and worked out. Athletes, writers, and artists often talk about being in this state of mind of following your instinct without question. They have referred to it as a trance-like state, being "in the zone," intimately connected to what they know is right.

When you feel stuck and indecisive, try to locate your bridal intuition and trust it. Ask yourself, *"What will make me smile on my wedding day?" "What will be fun?"* or *"What would make me and my fiancé happy?"* What comes up for you automatically? Which possibilities present themselves as naturally part of who you are and not derived through some other filter? The answers to these questions are usually quite clear and will allow each decision to feel more natural and less like pulling teeth. But you need to rely on that gut instinct and trust it.

Decisions Trick #3—Three Is the Magic Number

There are millions of photographers, venues, invitation styles and the like. You could easily drive yourself into an asylum by trying to research them all. Try narrowing your search down to three or whatever number works for you. It is easy to get overwhelmed with the countless options, and there is no need to consider more than three options for each of the decisions that you have to make.

Decisions Trick #4—Stick to Your Guns.

Once you have decided, and you are feeling good about it, trust yourself. Remember that there was a reason that you came to that decision, so do not allow there to be room to second-guess yourself. Move on to the next decision and let go.

Obsession Confession

Everyone has experienced a record, CD or even an iPod getting stuck on a song. It keeps repeating and repeating one part of the lyrics. Then it takes a special effort to help the music return to normal. Sometimes we get stuck with obsessions in the same way that a CD skips, and we need to just make an extra effort to move past this stuck place.

Obsessions can manifest in many forms whether you are going through a wedding or not. You may already get obsessed about things in your life, such as keeping your desk clean, serving the "right" wine for a dinner, or repeatedly replaying old conversations over in your head. When benign, obsessing can be considered a way of coping with worries, anxiety, and untapped energy. But when they reach a level where they are all-consuming, they need to be effectively managed.

It's no surprise that many women find themselves hyperfocused on something (or everything) in planning a wedding. If this rings true for you, rest assured that you are not alone. In fact, the stereotypical notion of an obsessed bride had to materialize from somewhere.

You may notice you are obsessed with a seemingly unimportant item like your wedding shoes, something you normally would not think twice about. You visit every store within a 25-mile radius, you troll websites at every little chance, and you comb through magazines to find the perfect pair. Perhaps you have seen another bride get obsessed over these little things, and now you find yourself doing it too.

The difficult part with obsessions is that you may be fully aware of being consumed by a particular aspect of your wedding, but you just can't seem to shake it. You know you are overly focused on your hairstyle, intensely preoccupied by the invitations, unnecessarily troubled by what your fiancé will wear, and overly intent on not having children at your ceremony. Yet, even though you intellectually know you are obsessing over these things, you still don't feel like you have the capacity or control to stop it. And as with some brides, you don't want to.

Assuming these obsessions are not seriously interfering with your day-to-day functioning in your work, your relationships, or your self-care (in which case, please ring a therapist), do not worry about them. These are transitory obsessions activated by an intrinsically chaotic and stressful event. Your obsessions are a symptom of this stress, and ironically they are a way you are trying to cope with it. They may be a natural way for you to protect yourself or cope with other, deeper feelings. And, being hyperfocused is not inherently bad. Many successful people achieve what they do by putting a great deal of focus on certain details. It is likely that your particular obsessions will pay off in some form.

In knowing this obsessive behavior is normal and

not interfering with your functioning, why not also redirect the energy to make it an asset for you? Play around with your internal CD player and get that song to stop skipping.

✿ ✿ ✿

Tina loved her very urban lifestyle. She was a highly motivated woman in pharmaceutical sales, excited beyond belief to have found the love of her life. Tina was also a lover of couture clothing, so finding the perfect wedding dress was a lifetime dream. Her search began by first taking her mom to shops all over town, and then it expanded with trips to San Francisco and New York to look at the latest designer gowns. Not yet content with what she had found, Tina proceeded to drag her friends around each and every weekend until she finally found the perfect one. The dress was everything she had ever dreamed of, French lace train, hand embroidered throughout, strapless yet not too revealing, low in the back, and comfortable enough to boogie in. It was without a doubt her dream dress. The only problem was the exorbitant price of $20,000. OUCH! Tina was certainly not poor but definitely not well-off enough to pay such a price for a one-day wear. But given the symbolism of this dress, it represented the fulfillment of a lifelong dream. Tina decided that she had to make it happen. She worked her tail off, putting in extra hours at her new company, ultimately fast-tracking herself to a huge promotion. In the end, Tina decided she loved the dress and the idea of a wedding more than her fiancé, so their engagement was broken off.

69

Yet, three years later, she was yet again engaged, this time to her best friend from childhood, a better match for her. There's no question what she wore to City Hall that September day.

✿ ✿ ✿

From the moment Cynthia saw the veil in a perfume ad, she could not imagine wearing any other. It was encompassed with delicate 1/2-inch lace and had a very subtle design embroidered within. It was old-fashioned but modern at the same time. She wanted it. She felt she needed it. She spent her lunch hour going to bridal stores searching for this exact veil. With no luck there, she soon found herself rummaging through fabric stores to find the perfect lace. At last she found it, but alas, the color did not match her dress. This only aggravated her obsession. She knew she was obsessed, yet, for whatever reason, the veil was so very important to her. It was her focus. She had crafted this notion that only if she had this veil would she feel extra fabulous on her wedding day. While faulty logic by any objective standard, this obsession was rather benign and still a source of pleasure rather than pain. Cynthia eventually had the veil replicated perfectly to the picture, and it was everything she had visualized. Yet, as irony would have it, a blustery wind blew it right from her head in the middle of the ceremony. Cynthia laughed and just stared in her husband's eyes, realizing that the veil was not that important to her.

✿ ✿ ✿

While we hope you feel normalized in how you perceive your obsessions, we would be remiss if we didn't mention another interpretation of obsessions, and one certainly with some merit. *Obsessions are oftentimes considered a creative way to deflect deeper emotional issues.* For instance, focusing on the flavor of the wedding cake is far easier than focusing on your feelings about being judged by your future in-laws. And obsessing over whether it will rain is a far safer place to sit than worrying about whether your estranged father will show up. You may want to ponder what deeper issue your obsessing may be masking. Tread lightly though, be gentle with yourself, and understand that this is all a symptom of stress.

CREATING A STRESS-FREE ZONE

We have gotten you to unveil your framework for your wedding, we have tackled the challenge of compromise, we have articulated tools for decision-making, and we have normalized your obsessions. All done? Well, not quite yet, because while all of these items will serve you well in your planning process, that's not to say they will eradicate the inherent stress involved.

It is a simple fact that stress is a part of the wedding process. And it is not just stress, but stress with a capital S. Few can avoid it, and it is hard to imagine a planning process that looks otherwise.

The aggravations can almost be considered mini rites of passage—the price doubles when you say the word "wedding," you need to order your dress months in advance, and you feel like you have to pay $900 for a cake that will likely only be nibbled at. Although we cannot change these nonsensical aspects of a wedding, they will feel more tolerable if you learn to manage your unwanted stress. And while stress can oftentimes be used effectively, too much stress is not good. Ultimately, your body, mood, and mind will begin to break down.

The Bridal Buddha ideas outlined in the second chapter are critical to defusing the stress you may feel as a bride. But there are also ways you can channel that stress into momentum, motivation, and excitement. Stress is the natural way we gear up to meet life's challenges. Essentially, you want to corral that stress, reframe it, and deploy it into a Wedding Stress-Free Zone.

Here's a 3-pronged approach to creating a Wedding Stress-Free Zone.

A little stress is good. It motivates you. It gets you to work. It helps you manage your sleep and hunger. It pushes you to order the cake and call your photographer. When you are a little stressed, your effectiveness is high and your mood is generally good and stable. If you are stressed enough to be excited and motivated, but not so stressed that you are overwhelmed and irrational, you are in the zone of high effectiveness and performance. You are in the wedding zone.

Schedule your stress. *Huh? Why would I want to actually schedule my stress?* A good question for certain and one deserving of an answer. Stress is an inescapable part of the wedding planning process, but that doesn't mean it needs to be a persistent part of it. Break up the destructive cumulative effects of stress into more manageable periods of it. This means scheduling your stress for a particular time of your week or of your day. By saying, *"Let's save our wedding to-dos and planning for Tuesday nights only from 7 to 9 pm,"* you have effectively gained control over it and have given yourself the freedom to feel the antidote to stress—calm—the rest of the week.

Schedule a break from your stress. What is the physical or psychological signal that tells you you are stressed? Everyone notices something different. Perhaps your mouth gets dry, your neck gets tight, a headache comes on, or you just feel plain cranky. Your specific symptom is a sign that it's time to take a few minutes to relax so you can get back in the wedding stress-free zone.

There may be things you already do to help you escape from stress. You may enjoy a glass of wine, hit the gym, or take a bath. The important thing is to *schedule* this break from stress and make sure it happens. By consciously focusing your efforts on diffusing your stress, your mind and body can relax in as quickly as four to six heart beats.

This 3-prong approach to stress puts you in the driver seat. It allows for a little stress to guide you, but it calls upon you to take a break from it, too. You have effectively entered the Wedding Stress-Free Zone.

Relationships: Managing the 3 F's Without Letting the "F" Word Sneak In

---

CHAPTER CONTENTS:

Digging Up The Dirt—Reliving Roles & Readjusting to New Ones

The 3 F's

Fiancé
Family—Building your bark
Friends

The Fix—Finding Empathy

I n an ideal world, your engagement would be about these 3 F's: fun, fanfare, and festivities. But in reality, the relational nature of a wedding brings to mind these 3 F's: fiancé, family, and friends. While you most certainly have warm fuzzy feelings about all three of these relationships, it is likely you will want to scream at least one of them at some point throughout your wedding planning process.

As has been similarly noted with emotions, the wedding process tends to amplify everything. The highs may be higher, and the lows may be lower. This holds true for your relationships as well. The tension you feel with your partner may increase. Your mom's watchful eye may become critical. Your brother may start to feel left out just like he did when you were eight and he was five years-old. Your best friend may become demanding and bossy like she was in middle school. Your dad may check out or get overly protective.

Even when family members have the best intentions, they may gravitate to old patterns and pre-set roles. Some of those behaviors may feel like a sock to the stomach, evoking images of years past, while others may feel just fine and nicely familiar. And new disturbing behaviors can unveil themselves, particularly in your more recent relationships, such as that with your fiancé. Complicating all of this even more is the fact that your loved ones crave *your* attention while you need people to attend *to you*.

While you may not have the emotional or physical energy to navigate some of these relationships during the height of wedding stress, the good news is that a wedding inherently endows you with a chance to *grow your roots*—essentially, you have the opportunity to enhance your connection to those closest to you and to gain a better understanding of the dynamics at play in these relationships.

Not to be too hokey, but in *growing your roots*, think of yourself as a tree. A tree is supported by its roots. The roots serve as a foundation, enabling it to grow strong and be steady. As a tree grows its roots deeper into the ground, the higher its branches can reach into the sky. Applying this metaphor to you as a bride, we can presume that the longer you grow your roots, the greater the risks you can take, and the more steady you will feel in the midst of conflict, tension, and disagreement. This is a chance to reframe the twists and turns of the past, develop more effective relationship dynamics, and achieve a new level of connection with yourself and with those around you.

Never in my life
Had I felt myself so near
That porous line
Where my body was done with
And the roots and the stems
And the flowers began.
                    White Flowers—Mary Oliver

DIGGING UP THE DIRT—RELIVING ROLES & READJUSTING TO NEW ONES

Interpersonal relationships can be the hardest part of an engagement. Zoë's story demonstrates this.

Zoë was a struggling artist, saving money for college and art school by working at the local bar. During the day she perfected her sculptures, building up her portfolio with the hopes of one day getting into the prestigious Chicago Art Institute. One night at the bar, a handsome guy named Nico walked in, ordered a round of drinks for himself and his roommate, and ultimately engaged Zoë in riveting conversation. The three of them discussed alternative bands they liked, explored politics and art, and connected on a level that felt unique and authentic. The discussion lasted late into the night, until finally Nico and Zoë decided to go out for breakfast the next morning, just the two of them. From that point forward each knew they had found their perfect match.

Nico proposed six months later.

However, the high from Zoë's engagement seemed to fizzle when she was around her mom. Growing up, her mom encouraged her to go to college, support herself, and after fully exploring her individuality and interests, maybe then it would be time to get married. Zoë's mom had always regretted getting married and pregnant at such a young age, believing she was never able to fulfill her own dreams of being a doctor. Now that her daughter was engaged, Zoë's mom was worried. She made subtle (and not so subtle) comments that suggested she did not approve of Zoë's engagement. She would constantly drop hints and throw out vague passive-aggressive comments that were obviously about her own experience and lost dreams. *"How are you going to go to school and be married?" "What about your dreams?" "So, I think the women's movement should really push further on how equal marriages are."*

Zoë's mom was projecting her history onto Zoë, subconsciously superimposing her desires onto her daughter. Amazingly, Zoë was very Zen about the whole thing, as it was quite clear what her mom was doing. Zoë was even able to interject a level of empathy when she felt caught up and frustrated by her mom's projections, and gently and thoughtfully discussed it with her. In the end, Zoë understood where her mom was coming from, and by putting on her wise emotional Buddha hat, she was able to separate her mom's dreams and projections from her own aspirations. Given that she couldn't count on her mom's miraculously seeing the light, Zoë found assurance and solace in the truth that *she was the only one who knew how she felt.* She effectively climbed out from the mess of parental projections and kicked those subtle family messages to the curb!

Weddings can be interpersonally unveiling. They can provoke a spectrum of ugly emotions for other people *even* if it is ostensibly a happy occasion for them too. Oftentimes those closest to us have a difficult time with what this rite of passage means to them, how this event may reflect on them, or what it may trigger for them about what's going in their own lives. Your family and friends may personalize your wedding and see it through the lens of what it means for them.

Your older sister, who just broke up with her serious boyfriend of four years, may have a far more difficult time with the reality of your wedding than your younger sister, who just kissed a boy for the first time. Your father may start to withdraw during your engagement and appear unsupportive, but really he is grappling with the meaning of his "little girl" getting married. And you may find your maid-of-honor to be suffocating, but she is really just trying to be the optimal support for the "sister" she never had.

What's happening is that people are projecting their own feelings and desires onto your process. The above examples of projecting speak to deep emotional conflicts, but projections can also manifest in petty ways. Your best friend wants a bridesmaid dress in her favorite color, not yours. "How could you pick red? Red is a horrible color. It makes me look pale." She is replacing your desires with her own. While your friends and family probably don't intend to rock the boat or cause you any angst, these projected comments and behavior come off as thoughtless, absurd, and at times just plain rude.

You could be in for some really rough moments if you aren't aware that these projections may be thrown your way with the full force of a semi-truck. *"I never liked that church." "A wedding is not a wedding without a cake."* However, if you are astute at assessing the dynamics at play, you will be able to brace yourself for the thoughtless and rude projections that seem to be inevitable in the wedding process.

Complicating these projections is the fact that everyone is trying to adapt to a new role. Not only are you trying to adjust to what being a bride means, those around you are trying to figure out their places as well. Your dad is no longer just "dad" but now "father-of-the-bride." Your boyfriend is not just your sweetie but both a "fiancé" and "groom." These are big and loaded titles, roles to which each person is not given very much time to adapt.

And of course, your role as "bride" is the biggest and the one for which we as a society harbor the most expectations. Unfortunately, your role is bigger than just planning a wedding. During this time, you are at the epicenter of all of these relationships. Your role has transcended the "planning task-master" and instead also involves being there for those whom you love and maintaining and growing these meaningful relationships—all while trying to do the virtually impossible task of putting your needs first. Here's another F for you, but a sarcastic one—fun!

THE 1ˢᵀ F—YOUR FIANCÉ

Of all of your relationships, your fiancé likely elicits the biggest smile, the most intense feelings of love and longing, and the greatest amount of excitement about what lies ahead for the two of you. But your fiancé is also likely your newest relationship and one that is still evolving. Given the meaning and magnitude of your wedding, new dynamics will be introduced as you each traipse (or stumble) through it all. If the wedding gods have blessed you, you may continue to fall more and more in love. But if you are like most, you will face new sets of challenges, ones that you will more than likely survive but that will feel derailing nonetheless.

Stuck—We Can't Agree, But We Can't Move on Either

Is there some topic you just cannot seem to agree on? Is it a topic you can't compromise on, like whether to invite children to the wedding? Or perhaps you want to have a big wedding and he wants to elope? You want to keep your name and he wants you to take his last name?

Now this may sound crazy but CONGRATULATIONS! You are both being honest. You are both expressing your truth and your genuine feelings about an issue.

On some level, we all lie to ourselves, and have fantasies that our lover sees everything exactly the way we do. Unfortunately, until you clone yourself, no partner, including your current fiancé, will ever see every single issue exactly the same way you do. However, it will help everyone if you continue to be honejulist to yourself and others, speak for your needs, let yourself be heard, and of course truly listen to your partner.

So you are now thinking, *"Great, we are being honest with one other, but we are still stuck!"*

Within relationships we often come across issues that feel like one person "wins" and the other person "loses and has to suck it up." However, working as a team and talking about each issue that falls into this stuck zone can really help. The research by the world-famous couples guru, Dr. John Gottman, suggests that when couples find the courage to open up about *why* they feel so strongly about an issue and try to understand where each is coming from, a creative solution often emerges. Sometimes this means that both partners end up compromising. Sometimes this means that one person's idea takes precedence over the other's. Regardless, it is not about compromising or winning. It is about building your ability to communicate and understand your partner's perspective. Do not keep score because that is when everybody loses.

Couples who are able to express their needs, dreams, and desires and also hear those of their partners are able to work through these gridlock issues. You may never agree, but by talking through the stuckness you will hopefully understand your partner's perspective. This will allow you to respect each other's differences and keep resentment at bay.

With this type of intimate communication, one partner may begin to see that while he may disagree, he does not hold the contested issue at such high importance as his partner does. This gives one partner the ability to give way to the other's needs. In addition, this increased communication and deference allows the other partner to acknowledge her loved one's sacrifice on this issue. This acknowledgement breeds togetherness. Plus, it allows the couple to work through the stuck zone and let go of any lingering resentments.

☼ ☼ ☼

Jennifer and Pete, a Chinese-American couple, were stuck on what kind of a wedding they wanted. Jennifer wanted to go to city hall and call it a day, or at the most have a small celebration in her backyard. Pete wanted to have the traditional huge Chinese wedding at a massive banquet hall. While they both understood *what* the other person wanted, they felt like one of them was going to have "give in" and let the other get his or her way. They were at a standstill.

Finally, they started to talk and really listen to *why* each had a particular preference. Jennifer, a successful biologist, did not want to spend the next year organizing a wedding for 500 people, taking time away from the things on which she really wanted to focus. Her dream was to receive a grant to lead a 6-week research expedition to Antarctica to study Penguins, not spend the next year researching font sizes for the invitations to be sent to every person her mother sees at the grocery store.

Pete on the hand, wanted to experience the ritual of the long ceremony, to show off his amazing bride to the world, and to respect his family and their traditions. He did not want to miss out on a once-in-a-lifetime opportunity to have everyone he knows together. Plus, he did not think he could face his parents to tell them about a city hall ceremony. His parents would feel that their marriage would be unlucky without a due celebration, and they would be very concerned for them.

After hearing one another's rationales, the solution came about. Jennifer did not feel like she was giving in when she said, *"let's have a big blow-out and make our parents happy."* She understood Pete's perspective and it meant more to him to have a big wedding than it did to her to elope. Pete also gained new knowledge, as he had had no clue she was so opposed to a traditional wedding for fear that it would potentially interfere with her career. To help ease her concern, he recognized that most of the wedding planning would fall on her, but he pledged to take as much off her plate as he could. Most importantly, he acknowledged the sacrifice she was making for them. His acknowledgement made it all feel worth it to Jennifer, as ultimately she was making Pete (and them as a couple) so happy.

A Matter of Values

Do you and your fiancé have the same values in life? Or do you disagree on religion, money, family, and kids? It is perfectly normal and acceptable if you don't agree, as most often this is the case. However, having different values often makes couples feel stuck and unable to come up with a compromise.

Having different values can feel confusing when disputes arise over the details of your wedding. You want religion to be a major focus of your ceremony and he does not even want the word "God" mentioned. You want your mom, dad, sister, and grandmother to be a significant part of your wedding day and your fiancé is not even excited about inviting his family. You want to discuss problems with him and he just wants to forget about them, seeming to hope they will disappear. While you may view shopping for your flower girl's dress as a fun activity, your fiancé cringes every time he even thinks about children.

The planning disputes between you and your fiancé may be endless, but fortunately they are usually surmountable when they are contained to just differences in opinion. But what happens when these disputes reveal significant differences in core values? Until now, your relationship may have not been challenged to unveil these value ruptures.

✩ ✩ ✩

Will and Christina are a great example of a groom and a bride who had mismatched values. They found themselves in a wedding debate over money and how it should be best used. Will wanted to have an open bar with top-shelf booze flowing until the wee hours. He remarked, *"It is the best celebration of our lives and I want to drink the good stuff that night. Plus I want my wedding to be an epic night that all of my friends remember."*

On the other hand, Christina could care less about any booze but was more focused on her attire. It was her lifelong dream to have a stunning wedding dress with a dramatic long train. Will's response— *"that's silly, it is just for one day—you will never wear it again."* Yet Christina mirrored his response stating, *"What you are going to drink the booze again the next day? That is only for one day too. At least I could pass down my dress to someone else!"*

Next came the discussion over whether to get a videographer. They went back and forth on the issue. Did they need everything on tape or was it an expense they could save on? They were both unsure. He wanted to bag the whole video idea. She thought she might regret not documenting this special day so she could look at it in the years to come.

In the end, Christina and Will realized that while they shared the value of thriftiness, they had different values about what *things* were actually worthy of money. Will and Christina acknowledged that they had different wants but concluded that it was okay. Instead of trying to control each other's spending, they chose to trust one another. Together with some compromises, they stayed within budget, got creative by having a friend videotape the wedding from a hand-held camera, and learned that they do not have to see eye-to-eye on everything.

✿ ✿ ✿

Different values can feel especially alarming when your and your fiancé's families start to take center stage and their differences are more intimately revealed. Perhaps your family is from New England, Jewish, loves to travel, and never talks about emotions. Perhaps his family is from Long Island, Catholic, loves to cook, and is very loud, especially at large family gatherings. While you each knew all of these familial traits before, these differences now seem to matter much more because you are planning your wedding from different perspectives.

✧ ✧ ✧

When Julia started her wedding planning, she was forced to take a closer look at some core value differences between her and her fiancé, Kevin. He was from a large Italian Catholic family. She not only loved him, but she also adored his family. Julia appreciated how he valued the importance of family and how their weekends were family-focused. She was not Catholic and never felt any pressure to attend church with them or convert until they got engaged.

Kevin's mother began asking how they were possibly going to get married if Julia didn't convert. *"But you have to get married in a Catholic church, right?!"* These comments made Julia feel very uncomfortable and she asked her fiancé to get his mom off her back. However, feeling intimidated by such a conversation, Kevin failed to confront his mother.

In the face of Kevin's unwillingness to stand up for Julia, she started to question the character of the man she was marrying. She was suddenly flooded with negative thoughts. Was Sunday dinner with his parents just a ploy to get his laundry done by his mom? Is he being passive and not addressing the "converting to Catholicism" conversation with his mom because he is actually on his mom's side? Has he not done any part of the wedding planning because he is just lazy? And why hasn't Kevin pushed back on his father's constant homophobic remarks that not only bother Julia but supposedly disgust him too? Julia began to wonder if Kevin's parents would always be his first priority.

At first Julia ignored all of these thoughts, as

she knew she loved Kevin. She also felt like she was way too deep into wedding planning to back out now: everyone who had already made arrangements to travel to her wedding, all the deposits to various vendors, the ridiculously expensive dress that already hung in her closet. Yet, she had trouble pushing these thoughts away. The more she seemed to have to nag Kevin to do any task related to the wedding, the more reasonable her concerns seemed. Moreover, every time Kevin felt overwhelmed with one of his wedding tasks, he would call his mom and ask for her opinion. This drove Julia nuts.

Julia had the courage to discuss her feelings with Kevin. Together they decided to attend a premarital workshop. At the workshop they listened to the married couple who led the seminar talk about how family-of-origin impacts the relationship, about communication and conflict resolution styles, as well as how to maintain sexual and emotional intimacy. They also spent time alone crafting letters to one another about their expectations for marriage, the challenges they fear, and their strengths as a couple. They then swapped letters, endowing each with a wealth of knowledge about the other. While the workshop did not fix all of their problems, it did bring individual concerns out into the open. They both agreed that Julia's worries about Kevin's enmeshed family could derail the relationship.

✿ ✿ ✿

As we stated earlier, couples who are clearly able to communicate their values and also hear those of their partners can work through conflict. Your values may never match up, but by talking through the differences you will hopefully understand your partner's perspective. This will allow you to respect each other's differences and work together to come up with solutions as a couple. Remember is it is not about winning or losing. It is about building your ability to communicate and understand your partner's perspective.

Premarital Finessing

You may cringe when you think about attending a premarital counseling weekend or a marriage prep class, but try to keep an open mind. Most couples (both men and women) walk away from these weekends jazzed and thankful they devoted the time to it. It can be another way to further solidify the foundation you have already built. Plus, it can help bring awareness to any hot-spots you may have with your partnership, hear directly what your fiancé appreciates about you, and unveil any major value differences that could be potential roadblocks.

These workshops do not have to be through your church; many non-religious classes and seminars are offered by professional counselors as well.

Managing Your Man (And Better Yet, Your Expectations)

Planning a wedding brings out the taskmaster and control-freak in even the most mild-tempered women. These beasts rear their heads most frequently with the one person who actually deserves to have a voice in your wedding—your fiancé. You may want to plan this wedding together, but your fiancé can barely look up from the TV when it's time to discuss it. You want to give him some autonomy to choose things that may be important to him, but you don't trust his follow-through. You are left feeling disappointed and frustrated on how to attain a balance between independence (and subsequent action) and togetherness (and subsequent inertia).

During your engagement, it is natural to want your fiancé to be superman. However, if you hold him to an A-plus standard in every category, you are setting yourself up for disappointment and setting him up for failure.

Moreover, we doubt in return that you want to live up to his superwoman standards. He may want a hot three-course meal every night, but there is just no way you can manage that when you are working full-time and planning a wedding. During your engagement, keep some realistic expectations for each other, and you may both be able to keep your sanity.

A key piece of the relationship puzzle is *picking your battles*. And just as any effective warrior has a game-day strategy, you need to know exactly what it is that you want/need/expect before you engage in the battle.

Here are some general guidelines when trying to effectively and humanely communicate:

1. Remember, ambiguity can be a death wish, figuratively speaking of course. Do not be vague.
2. Make sure your want/need/expectation is reasonable and achievable.
3. Communicate in clear concrete terms.

For example, let's say you have reached your max when it comes to wedding tasks. You are not sure you have the energy to tackle the flowers, and you really wish your fiancé would help out and realize that he hasn't done squat yet. Well, this may be a time to *pick your battle.* You could say to him, *"I know you could care less about the flowers, but I am feeling overwhelmed with all this wedding stuff and I need your help. I will make the arrangements for the bouquets. But can you please e-mail me how many boutonnieres we need for your friends and family by next Monday?"* This request is clear, direct, reasonable, and most certainly achievable.

Another strategy that you could employ throughout your engagement is to ask your fiancé to do one small thing each week; this will prevent any resentments on your part and let you know that he is paying attention. If it's in the planning realm, perhaps he can create a list of three potential bands. If it's in the relational realm, let him know in no uncertain terms that you are craving more connection and that you would appreciate a date night. Again, do not be vague: ask for exactly what you need.

In the beginning, however, it is smart to start with small requests that won't overwhelm him—you want to set him (and you!) up for success. And be sure to make room for reciprocity, too; have your fiancé ask you for one small specific thing that he needs to show him that you are paying attention to his needs as well.

This whole exercise helps in managing expectations, a crucial ingredient to relational satisfaction, not only during your wedding but also for your lifetime. This process will naturally help you focus on what is working in the relationship, so you can do more of it. And if done well, the little things may lead to even bigger gains.

Staying Connected—Finding New Ways To Show Your Affection

The love between you and your fiancé is similar to a fire. Not only does it require constant tending, but like a relationship, it is easier to keep a fire burning than to re-create it from scratch. Adding layers of kindling helps build the foundation and allows for continuity.

Your wedding presents yet another challenge in the relational realm, as it can often interfere with that fire of connection between you and your fiancé. But by effectively and consistently communicating your love and affection, you are giving the fire more air and fuel to burn. It keeps the fire steadily burning.

Despite your stress, despite the never ending to-do lists, and despite the tugs for attention from your family and friends, *now* is a perfect time to develop habits that will communicate to your fiancé that you love him. Just as with your wedding, you will face other stressful transitions throughout your marriage. However, these trying times cannot be used as devices for dismissing and downplaying the need for affection. In fact, these are the times when we need *more* love and affection, especially from those closest to us.

Consider this your invitation to pour on the affection towards your fiancé. Challenge yourself to find new ways to show your love. Be expressive in your gratitude and appreciation. Do not close the door on fun, but rather uncover different channels for you to share joy. Be creative, be adventurous, be bold.

If you tend to show him affection verbally, try enhancing tenderness through touch, perhaps by holding his hand in the middle of dinner. If you are more comfortable being expressive in the bedroom, put post-it love notes all over his closet door, buy him his favorite magazine, write "I Love You" on the bathroom mirror with lipstick. Seize the little moments where you can sneak in some affection. Walk him to his car before work, send him off with an intimate kiss. Leave him a love note in his wallet, pack him a lunch, compliment the way he told a story, do the dishes even after you cooked dinner. We are not trying to turn you into a 1950's housewife, but rather remind you of the importance and power of these simple moments of affection.

Cheat Sheet For Affection

Relationship expert, Dr. Gary Chapman, is the author of *The Five Love Languages* (1995) Zondervan. In this book he writes about the importance of being able to express love to your mate in a way that he can understand. Dr. Chapman calls this type of communicating the Five Love Languages:

Words of Affirmation: These are verbal expressions of appreciation, love, and affection that are intended to communicate *I love you*. This is saying how nice your spouse looks or how great the dinner tasted. These words will also build your mate's self-image and confidence.

Quality Time: Some spouses believe that being together, doing things together, and focusing on one another is the best way to show love. If this is your partner's love language, stop reading your favorite wedding blog and give one another some undivided attention.

Gifts: It is a universal behavior in human cultures to give tangible objects showing affection. They don't have to be expensive to convey a powerful message of love.

Acts of Service: This means doing some task, chore, service that will benefit your partner. It may require some time and creativity, like picking up his dry cleaning, getting his car washed, doing all the research for the honeymoon, or doing something that was originally deemed "his wedding job." These acts need to be done with joy and devoid of any quid-pro-quo expectation in order to be perceived as an act of love.

Physical Touch: Sometimes just stroking your spouse's back or a peck on the cheek will fulfill this need. Couples tend to underestimate how much their partner is craving physical attention.

But how do you determine your partner's love language? People communicate love to their partner in the way they want their partner to communicate it to them. (Chapman, 1995) Pay attention to how your fiancé communicates love to you. Perhaps he tends to massage your feet while you are watching TV (physical touch). This is his love language. If you want to communicate your love to him, try rubbing his shoulders before bed. Speaking in your spouse's love language probably won't be natural or easy for you, particularly if yours is quite the opposite. Dr. Chapman says, "We're not talking comfort. We're talking love. Love is something we do for someone else. So often couples love one another but they aren't connecting. They are sincere, but sincerity isn't enough."

This is a unique time requiring unique overtures, which will likely lay the foundation for your marriage. Open up your creative mind and show your affection in as many ways as you can. Keep that fire burning.

Cold Feet

Often brides feel apprehensive before their wedding, wondering, *"Is this the guy for me?"* A part of that fear and uncertainty may be excitement and nervous tension; these feelings are natural and normal. A little doubt and a discerning heart are a good sign in the midst of any major life decision. After all, you are about to enter into a formal, legal commitment by getting married, and given its significance, you might as well allow yourself some space to massage your decision a bit.

Tamyra and her fiancé Dan had handled the majority of the details for their wedding weekend, from the venue to the DJ, the cake, the food, and the little touches that would make their ceremony memorable. It was challenging, but they made the best of it. Tamyra's mother, a busy lawyer, was thrilled her daughter was taking the reins. However, Dan was an only child, and his mother had been dreaming of his wedding day for a long time. She really wanted to be involved in the planning. In turn, Tamyra and Dan gratefully allowed his mother to be in charge of selecting and ordering the flowers.

On the day of her wedding, Tamyra stopped by

the reception venue to pick up the bridal party flowers. Her hair and makeup were already done, and she only had a few minutes before heading to the church. The centerpieces and bouquets for the bridesmaids looked fantastic, but where was the bouquet for the bride? The florist showed her the order form for 14 center pieces and 3 bridesmaid's bouquets. *"Oh my goodness!"* she gasped. *"Dan's mother forgot to order my bouquet. What a Freudian slip,"* she thought, based on her mother-in-law's tendencies. While Dan's mother struggled with sharing her son, this was a ridiculous mistake.

The venue they picked for the wedding was out in the countryside, therefore isolated. There was no way to get more flowers at this point. Tamyra's heart sank. She called her husband-to-be. *"Dan, thank God you picked up. Your stupid mom forgot to order a bouquet for me. Can you believe it?...What? Don't call your mom stupid?...What? You think I forgot to put the bride's bouquet on the list for the florist? Are you kidding?"*

Tamyra felt a wave of anger and was flooded with memories of romantic evenings spoiled by interrupting phone calls from Dan's mother. The Bridal Buddha in her had initially believed that all would be okay, but she was not expecting Dan's defensive tone. All she wanted was a moment of compassion from her groom and instead she got attitude. She hung up and panicked, asking herself, *"how can I marry a man who still talks to his mom each night? I cannot let myself do this. What am I doing?"* She pictured herself hopping in her car, driving far, far away, and never coming back. It was not too late. She could still escape. *Was she having cold feet?* Tamrya's escape plan fantasy was interrupted by something tugging on her leg. It was her flower girl dressed and ready. She looked absolutely adorable and she was grinning ear to ear. *"Aunty Tamyra where is your big white dress?"* Tamyra reached down and kissed her on the forehead. In that moment she knew everything was going to be alright. And to reinforce this feeling, Dan was calling. *"Dan?....Awww. Thanks hon for understanding why I would be so upset. It is going to be ok. I am sorry I barked and called your mom stupid. She didn't do this on purpose. We will figure something out. Perhaps the florist can make three bouquets into four."*

The date of Debbie's wedding was rapidly approaching, and the mounting pressure made her feel apprehensive. She walked into her therapist's office a week before moving in with her fiancé and a month away from her ceremony. She was panicking: *"I need more time. I feel rushed and I question all of this."* As she dove deeper into her feelings, Debbie revealed, *"He is so different from my friends."* When her therapist asked her what she meant by different, Debbie said, *"Well, he does not really have that silly gene, the goofy way I can be with some of my friends."* The more Debbie continued to piece together her feelings with her therapist, the more she fixated on his lack of goofiness. *"I just don't know if I want to marry someone who doesn't make me laugh like that."*

At the same time, Debbie felt a lot of pressure

and that it was too late to go back on her word. At the end of the hour, her therapist gave Debbie some feedback and reminded her that pressure can often often lead to resistance. *"Take away all this pressure and you may feel differently. You can always give yourself some more time. What is most important is making the right decision. Second, you are not making this decision alone. It may be the hardest thing you do, but try talking to your fiancé. You got into this together."* Debbie left feeling a bit better, but with tears running down her face. She wondered how she could ever talk to him about this, basically critiquing his personality.

The next week, Debbie relayed to her therapist that she had asked him for more time. *"I was scared, but I asked him anyway. In doing so, I realized how patient and understanding he always is. This is one of the things I have always cherished about him, and I have never found this quality in any other guy I have dated. He may not have as much of a goofy gene as me or my friends, but after talking to him I realized that is what I need from my husband. I love him just the way he is."* Debbie paused, smiled, and then continued. *"Oh, and by the way, I moved in with him last weekend, and I love our new place. I also wrote the most wonderful vows to say to him in our ceremony."* In affording herself permission to slow down, Debbie was no longer feeling the pressure and was able to move forward.

✧ ✧ ✧

Many brides start to feel like it is "too late" to discuss concerns with their fiancés. Usually this is around worrying about money already spent or people already committed. *It is important to remember that no matter how many deposits you have made or how much your future in-laws have invested in the wedding, it is never too late.*

☼   ☼   ☼

Trudy sat in her car before going into what would have been her third couples counseling appointment with her fiancé. They had been together for six years, and her wedding was a month away. Trudy felt a pit in the bottom of her stomach. Her whole body ached. Something was wrong, but she just couldn't figure it out until that very moment when it suddenly came to her. Trudy realized that she was not going to counseling to fix her relationship, she was hoping the therapist would help her end her relationship.

This huge aha moment was difficult to take in, and she felt nauseous. She had finally discovered the reason she felt so detached, blasé and constantly irritable at her fiancé, but she thought telling him would absolutely destroy him.

Somehow she pulled herself together and walked into her counselor's office. With tears streaming down her face and her body shaking, she told him. *"I don't think I want us to work. I don't think we are meant to be together for the rest of our lives."* The counselor wanted to explore further to make sure it was not just a case of nerves, but it was quite clear that Trudy had more than just cold feet. She needed to bail.

Years later, Trudy looked back and realized that it was the hardest decision of her life, yet perhaps the best. It was absolutely agonizing to break her fiancé's heart and to tell all the closest people in her life that her wedding was off. And yet, despite her greatest fears, ending the engagement did not destroy her ex-fiancé. In fact, soon after he married a woman who far better suits him, and they have a baby on the way. Trudy is forever thankful she listened to her gut instincts.

✧   ✧   ✧

Some brides find it helpful to think of their engagement as a test. This does not mean simply passing or surviving the engagement process. Instead, it is about determining whether this marriage is right. Many brides have called off their weddings just hours before and were so grateful they did. It is never too late.

Ideally of course, your engagement will endow you with more evidence that confirms your choice of a life partner. But it can also be an opportunity to uncover evidence to the contrary. The challenging part is discerning which doubts are cause for concern and which doubts are simply reflections of the tension you and your fiancé feel in planning a wedding.

You know your relationship better than anyone else, as well as what made you to fall in love. We offer the following as guidelines for helping you warm up those cold feet.

Non-Negotiable Red-Flags

First and foremost, let's rule out any big red flags. Any verbal, emotional and physical abuse should not be accepted and should be serious cause for concern. Abuse can start subtly, but it is insidious and can reap disaster on your mental and physical health. Pay attention to your intuition; your gut will tell you if you are in a tenuous relationship. If you neglect any serious concerns, they may end up growing bigger and even more complex, imperiling you with potentially disastrous consequences. Please do not expect serious concerns to magically change after your wedding day.

✿ ✿ ✿

Signs of a Troubled Relationship

In your heart you may already know if he is "it" or if you truly need to "quit." This list from Daphne Rose Kingma's book *Coming Apart* (2000) Conari Press, may help you determine whether you are seeing the signs of the end of your relationship and not the beginning of a healthy marriage.

Here are some indicators that your relationship may be coming apart:

1. Fighting. Other than some rare sparkling moments, has your relationship turned into World War III or is it just a constant battleground? Some fighting is a sign of a healthy relationship. Yet, if you are having repetitive non-productive fights that do not end in feeling emotionally closer, this may be a form of ending a relationship.

2. Irreconcilable Differences. Yes, this is the infamous term for celebrity divorces, but more importantly it may be a sign your relationship is headed south too. When you first met, perhaps you and your fiancé agreed on everything. Yet, what you agree on seems to be less and less. Now you wonder how you even agree on the same toothpaste.

3. Boredom. Yes, boredom may mean you are actually tired, disconnected, and blue. You may just feel like you are in a "blur" or the relationship lacks passion. The two of you may have turned away from each other and now you feel a lack of excitement within yourself or the relationship.

4. Emotional Distance. Do you feel more connected with your Facebook friends than your fiancé? You may rationalize by saying *"we need to just work on our communication."* But this is similar to boredom; you are avoiding what the detached feeling is really about, slowly moving away from each other emotionally.

5. Changes in Venue. Geographical and domestic circumstances can have a major impact on the relationship. You may think, *"We were great until he started medical school and we moved to Boston."* This change in venue may feel innocuous, but it should be taken seriously.

6. Affairs. An affair may unconsciously be a means to end the relationship. Often people do not know they are at the end or know how to end a relationship. Affairs are not always the end, but

often they can be indicators of the emotional truth.

7.   Counseling & Therapy. Unfortunately, some couples come to therapy either to break up or at a point when the relationship is beyond repair. By no means is this always the case, as many people seek therapy as a resource to get that extra boost their relationship needs. However, therapy can be a sign of the unconscious reality that the couple wants to end the relationship.

✿ ✿ ✿

Quirk vs. Quack

Ironically, as you contemplate spending the rest of your life with the man you love the most, his quirky habits may start to really bother you. Things that used to bother you just a little now seem monumental. And things you never noticed before your engagement start to build to almost unbearable frustration. One bride was frustrated by the way her husband-to-be brushed his teeth. Another fixated on her fiancé's hours at work. One bride started criticizing her partner's late night ice cream runs. It is almost too easy to start worrying about your fiancé (and his habits) when you are really the one who is feeling anxious inside.

The first remedy for this quandary is to remind yourself that your annoyances are often symptomatic of your anxiety. Just as you have realized that others are projecting onto you, you are projecting your anxiety onto your fiancé. If you are hungry, stressed, tired, or emotionally drained, it's a sure-fire guarantee that his habits will start to drive you nuts. When you feel yourself frustrated, do the Bridal Buddha—pause, take a step back, breathe, and notice what is going on before you say something. Reacting in the moment can lead to hurtful words and miscommunication. Wait until you are in a neutral state of mind and embark on a clear, thoughtful, non-blaming, and rational discussion.

But even if you handle your reactions correctly, you still need to discern whether your fiancé's behavior is simply a *quirk* or representative of a *quack*. While the language we use may be light, the implications are not. Are these things that you can learn to love (or at least accept), or are these behaviors more indicative of aspects you wonder whether you can tolerate for the long term. Categorize what's bothering you into these two camps—quirkiness versus quackiness—and while life should generally be thought of in shades of gray, a concrete log can help you decide whether your worry is merited.

The Wise Third Party

Modern day couples counseling evolved from premarital counseling that was traditionally offered by the church. Whether you are religious or not, this practice has survived for generations for a reason. Seeking out the advice of an experienced and supportive third party can be the solution you need to your relational symptoms. If you are feeling confused and uncomfortable, definitely schedule some time with a church leader or a psychotherapist. Given that you are planning a wedding, you don't have the luxury of time to mess around with ambivalence.

While the sensation of cold feet is normal and

has a specific purpose, you do not want to ignore the things that are really bothering you in the relationship. Although compelling, it is not acceptable to think that your relationship will drastically change after you get married. Additionally, repression can lead to erratic behavior, self-destructive coping mechanisms, and sometimes depression. Tending to your relationship tangles now will help you learn how to untie them, affording you a healthy space devoid of resentments and ensuring a better relationship foundation on which to commence your marriage.

THE 2ND F—FAMILY

Your challenge during this time is to not only transition into your new role as bride but also grow into a woman individuated from your family. This transition into what psycho-babble calls *differentiation* involves two pieces—first, finding your voice by setting reasonable boundaries, and second, moving beyond entrenched family roles and relational patterns and developing new ones that will take you into this next phase of your life.

✿ ✿ ✿

Lauren was in her residency at a prestigious hospital in Atlanta when she got engaged. Given her crazy schedule, she had neither the desire or the time to plan her wedding. Her mother, on the other hand, had been dreaming of this day since Lauren was born. Lauren did not want the big Southern reception, the white dress, or the church wedding, but she also did not have the time or the energy to argue with her mother, rationalizing that it was just one day and her mother could be in charge.

Every few weeks, her mom would call and relay all the details of the wedding planning. Lauren's only request was to have a lemon wedding cake. However, her mother ignored her daughter's request and, in the end, picked out a wedding cake that was her favorite: white cake with raspberry filling. Lauren was utterly disappointed. In her work at the hospital she negotiated difficult situations and people all the time; yet she was unable to get the person who should be her closest ally to compromise on the one thing she wanted—a lemon wedding cake.

To Lauren's surprise, just two weeks before her wedding, a few of her friends at the hospital threw her a shower with a mini lemon cake. The cake was delicious and Lauren was touched by the fact that her "work family" in Atlanta had been paying attention and had managed to thoughtfully surprise her with the lemon cake she had always wanted.

✿ ✿ ✿

Building Your Bark—Finding Your Voice in the Vortex of Your Family

The bark of a tree is what protects it, enabling it to live in the elements of nature. While a tree may be part of a deep system of roots, it stands on its own, an individual entity apart from its foundation. *Building your bark* is about differentiating yourself from your family-of-origin, and planning a wedding provides you with a unique opportunity to do as much. While there is an organic piece to differentiation—it naturally happens on its own—there is also a piece that requires your conscious effort.

As an independent woman, you likely want to be an integral part of your family, but you also want to be our own person. It may feel like these drives are diametrically opposed—maintain your family relationships in all their richness *or* get your own needs met, but not both at the same time. Moreover, since family is an extension of self, you may have a tendency to make huge personal sacrifices to keep connected with them. Although you may not have it any other way, it's critical to assess whether the complicated dynamics of your family have caused you to lose touch with your own desires, overly identify with the feelings of your family, and ultimately find it impossible to say "no."

Building your ability to say "no" and "I care" at the same time is not only about finding your voice, but also about setting reasonable boundaries, differentiating yourself from your family. It is increasing your ability to identify your own reality, express your internal thoughts and feelings, while remaining close to those dearest to you. It's rooting out that impulse to please, squashing the voice that sounds like that of your parents, and saying *"I love you, but this is who I am and this is what I want."*

You may be thinking that this all sounds nice and well, but you can't imagine enacting it. Right now, you may feel like your two choices are to (a) blow up and hurt your family's feelings, or (b) repress your needs and cater to your family. Perhaps you know your family all too well, and they just don't work in these shades of gray. However, we are here to say that people respond to what you put out there. You don't need to either lash out or to repress. You can indeed find the middle ground of saying "no" and "I care" at the same time, and we promise, your family will ultimately get it.

There are so many ways this process can play out with your family as you plan a wedding. Let's imagine you want a kid-free wedding instead of a one with a million screaming children running around, but of course, your mother does not approve. She calls you up to explain, *"I do not have the heart to tell your cousins that they can not bring their children to your wedding. Besides, a wedding is not a wedding without children running around! Do you have a problem with children these days?"* You could easily take your mother's opinion as a personal attack on your taste. You may feel like lashing out at her, bursting into tears, or hanging up the phone.

What if you could say "no" and "I care" at the same time? The conversation may go differently if you are able to separate and identify your own internal reality (the comment hurt your feelings, but you know you feel strongly about having a kid-free event while still staying in contact with your mother. You could say: *"Mom, I know you have always pictured children at your daughter's wedding, and I respect that. But Tom and I have thought this through. We would really like a peaceful adult event that is an opportunity for my cousins to have a romantic night out without their kids. This is really important to us."* This kind of response not only takes care of the relationship by acknowledging your mother's feelings, but it also takes care of yourself. You protect your space and your opinions without damaging the relationship. You hear your mother's feedback and remain close with her without getting caught up in her opinion—all without even having to actually say the word "no"!

The more familiar you are with your own personal limits, the easier it is to say "no" and inoculate yourself from automatically falling back into a parent-pleasing mode and habitually saying "yes."

So, what are your limits? A big question for sure, but one that is made easier by putting it into context. Your limits are dynamic, shifting as a result of the *person*, your *emotional resources*, and the *situation*.

Your ability to say "no" may fluctuate depending on the *person* with whom you are interacting. There may be some family members to whom you can never imagine saying "no" (you will gladly cater to your beloved grandma's wish to have you wear her tattered veil) and others for whom the "no" easily rolls off your tongue (your little brother's request to break-dance for you). You may tremble at the thought of saying "no" to your father but think you can find the courage to turn down your mother. Knowing where you stand in relation to each of your family members helps in navigating this oftentimes treacherous terrain towards differentiation.

Your *emotional resources* have an impact on your ability to set limits as well. If you are feeling energetic, fresh from a workout, you may be able to handle a conversation with your mom about Aunt Martha's outfit options for the rehearsal dinner. You may deftly maneuver the conversation to get the answer you want. However, if you are under a deadline at work and feeling stressed and pressed for time, you may be unable to say "no." Don't set yourself up for failure by entering into discussions when you aren't emotionally refreshed.

The *situation* also makes a huge difference with regard to limits. Some people have a hard time stating feelings in a group situation, but have no problem opening up one-on-one. Alone with your mom, you freely can say, *"Mom this is the dress I love. Please stop telling me that you want something that looks more traditional or Vera Wangish."* However, at a bridal salon, under the eyes of many strangers, it can be hard to muster up the courage to say something.

The emotional consequences of not setting limits with your family, particularly during your wedding, can be disastrous. Not only are you reinforcing your old roles of deference, but your wedding process may be colored by negativity. You may end up feeling resentful, exhausted, or angry. Devoid of advocating for yourself, you may even start to feel depressed, misunderstood, or devalued.

While it may be hard to imagine how a difference in opinion on something as trivial as a wedding cake could wreak such havoc on your emotional well-being, remember this process is reflective of your ability (or inability) to *build your bark* and ultimately find your voice within the vortex of your family. This is about seizing this opportunity to lay the foundation for new family patterns moving forward. Your wedding is a launching pad for a more enhanced and independent you.

✿ ✿ ✿

Michelle's parents divorced when she was 13 years-old. Since the bitter court battle, her parents had only been in the same room twice—at her high school graduation and at a funeral. Michelle had hoped that they could put their differences aside for her wedding, but she knew that might be impossible.

Although Michelle had involved her mom in the wedding planning, paid for her plane ticket, and reserved her a room, Michelle's mother hadn't sent in her RSVP card. One week before the wedding, Michelle asked her mother who she preferred to sit by at the reception and her mother dropped the bombshell—she wasn't coming. *"I am sorry Michelle, but there is no way I can sit there with your father and his new plastic, arm candy, trophy-wife."*

Michelle was utterly devastated and shocked by her mom's decision. She hung up and let this bombshell sink in. She felt like she was back in high school again, managing the conflicts between her parents. Michelle knew how much her mother hated being around her dad, and yet she also knew that having her mom at her wedding was really important to her. After a few hours of calming down and rejuvenating, she called her mom and was able to convince her to come. Michelle rationally encouraged her mother to put her feelings towards her dad aside for just that weekend and helped her mom understand the hurt that would she would have to endure if her mother skipped out on her wedding.

Michelle's father, on other hand, asked his daughter if it would be okay if he made a toast at both the rehearsal dinner and the reception. He took his needs to the next level but also asked if he could invite his three golfing buddies and their wives. Plus, her new stepmother asked if she could bring her own friend so she would feel more comfortable facing Michelle's mother. Michelle nicely said, "yes" to the reception toast but otherwise firmly said "no, no and NO." Michelle's father was a really difficult person to turn down, but she knew she had to or she would end up feeling resentful.

As if the pre-wedding parental difficulties weren't enough to handle, once Michelle's mother and father got into town they proceeded to complain non-stop. They grumbled that Michelle liked the other parent better, that she was not spending enough time with them individually, that it was too humid. They questioned why her brother wasn't in the wedding, and why Michelle wasn't letting children come to the reception or wedding. The negative chatter from both sides was out of control.

However, Michelle was very Buddha-like and let the noise bounce off her. She knew her parents were just anxious and uncomfortable. She had spent a lifetime trying to fix their marriage or at least reconcile it within her head. These years of experience in dealing with her parents' antics paid off, as Michelle let the comments and the conflict go. As an adult and a woman about to embark on her own family, it was no longer her job to be stuck in the middle.

Despite the familial hassles, Michelle absolutely loved every minute of her wedding. And *because* of her familial history, Michelle has a keen sense of who she is as a person, ultimately allowing her to find her life partner and love her husband even more.

✿　✿　✿

Dealing with Divorced Parents

Family matters are complicated enough during any bride's engagement. Unfortunately, the dynamics of a divorce amplify the already complicated family drama. All too often parents have not worked through the loss of their own marriage, even though it may have been years since the divorce. And at times, it may seem like your parents are reverting to their old antics of trash-talking one another or whomever the other happens to now be dating. You find yourself feeling like a child again, pressured to choose sides or, even worse, forced to mediate communication between the two.

A great example of a mom's unresolved loss is portrayed in the story of Lilly and Ben. One weekend Lilly's mom came to town for business and took Lilly and her fiancé Ben out to brunch. When the discussion turned to wedding details, her mom abruptly blurted, *"You know having your father walk you down the aisle is a sham. He gave you away when you were five years-old and left us. I know it is traditionally that way but still! Your stepfather Bill and I are paying for half of this wedding. Can't Bill and I give you away or at least have a say in all of this?"* Lilly politely chimed in, *"Mom, of course you have a say, but let's remember it is still my wedding. I hear what you are saying, but I still would like my dad to walk me down the aisle."* Although Lilly was impressed with her ability to rationally speak up to her mom, she still sat dumbfounded. She was amazed that her mother, 10 years after separating from her father, was still says things like this.

Divorced parents may feel a tinge conflicted about their daughter getting engaged. On one hand, they may feel pure excitement at such momentous news. On the other hand, it may also bring up their greatest fear—not only being in the same room with their ex-spouse after so many years but also having to feign politeness. But as much as it can stir up feelings for them, it can also stir up feelings for you. You may even feel similar to when they were first separated. If you were in early childhood when they divorced, you may have felt like it was your fault and held onto a lot of anxiety. If you were older, you may have just been pissed off. These feelings may re-emerge now. Still, as an adult, *it is not your job to heal your parents' wounds of their divorce.* And although you rationally know this, let us restate: *it is not your fault* that they separated. And during your engagement, it is not *your* responsibility to mend their fences; that is *their* parental duty.

Each parent must heal himself and herself. As much as you may want to try, you cannot do it for them. However, you do have the opportunity to pave a different role for yourself. Try speaking up for what you want now (something that was likely impossible as a child). For example, gently request that you not be the communication mediator or kindly ask them to refrain from badmouthing the other parent while you are present. Trying to change your dynamic in this situation may even aid them with their healing.

☼ ☼ ☼

Diane's wedding story is an all too-realistic example of how divorce and budgetary stress can be a dreaded combination. Diane and her father were exceptionally close. Together they began to plan for an elaborate father-daughter dance at the reception. Six months before the wedding, they began a weekly dance class that would help them build out their routine.

One night, while telling her father about a wedding dress she had found, Diane's father questioned, *"Your mother is not helping with one dime of the wedding, is she?"* Diane just continued dancing, hoping he was simply talking to himself. Yet, he continued, *"You know that I don't think she ever spent any of thousands I gave her in child support on you when you were younger. Now I am sure she will not spend any of her alimony on your wedding either. She can be so self-centered, I'm so sorry I married her, and I am just sorry that you don't have a better mother. Anyways, how much is this dream dress going to cost me?"*

Diane felt such a range of feelings from her dad's diatribe —guilt about the cost of the wedding, anger towards her father for talking so negatively about her mother, irritation that her mother was not pitching in (even though she knew money was tight for her), and sadness that her mother continued to be emotionally and physically absent during her engagement. Deep down, in some ways, Diane just wished that her parents had worked harder on their relationship and had never gotten a divorce in the first place.

Diane decided she needed to be brave and speak her truth, share her feelings with her father. Diane let her father know how awful it was when he talked so cynically about her mother and how guilty she felt about the money he was spending on her wedding.

Her father couldn't have reacted more supportively. Diane was relieved to hear that her dad was just teasing about the alimony and that he had set aside money for her wedding and her wedding dress years ago—money that he genuinely wanted to Diane to enjoy now. Diane had no idea that speaking her truth would ultimately prevent his tendency towards criticism or help him understand her perspective, but regardless she felt leaps and bounds better after letting him know where she stood.

✧ ✧ ✧

On top of the unresolved loss, divorce inherently invites practical and logistical variables—estranged parents, new significant others, step-children, and family members who no longer speak. These divorce variables impact everything from the invite list to seat assignments to budget. It can be very tricky to define the roles of various family members (blood-related or step) and to manage the feelings that these potential old wounds hold for you. Many brides struggle with situations like having both a step-mother and a mother in the same room at the bridal shower, figuring out whether step-siblings are automatic shoo-ins to be in wedding party, or trying not to "favor" one parent over the other.

Divorce is a thorny subject no matter how you slice it. For many brides, it may make them question if they will end up like their parents—divorced. As an adult, you may expect to be over it and perhaps you are. However, if you are not, and you are feeling hurt, angry and lost, please know you are not alone. Divorces as well as the feelings and memories they evoke are tremendously difficult to manage when you are planning a wedding. We hope that the general strategies, ideas, and bridal narratives in this section can be help you better cope and navigate the potential messiness of your divorced family.

Taking a Magic Wand to Your Family!

Whether your family is intact or your parents are divorced, you are forced to confront an array of different familial issues during your engagement. You thought you were just getting married, right? Not so simple. All of your relationships and their various facets have tentacles that reach far into your emotional being, complicating your best efforts to simply plan a darn wedding.

Just like coming home for the holidays, family patterns don't tend to change much. Yet they can. However, the only thing you can control and change is yourself, and by changing yourself, your family is then forced to change. Let's use a metaphorical magic wand and apply it to your family in a step-by-step process.

1. Ask yourself some questions to assess the relationship patterns.

Let's say you are feeling overwhelmed with wedding planning. While this is certainly a normal and common sentiment, this sensation of being overwhelmed may affect each of us differently based on our family histories. Ask yourself some questions:

- How did your family and friends cope with stress?
- What kind of modeling for stress management did you grow up with?

- How did your loved ones react to you when you were stressed?
- Did they comfort you, ignore you, or try to control you?
- How have you handled stress in the past? Has that method worked?
- Who has *really* been able to help you when you are stressed?
- In the past, what kind of insecurities did you feel about yourself when you were stressed?
- What worked to calm you?

Reflecting back on these old relationship dynamics can reveal many powerful insights—who you should turn to in the face of stress, how people will probably act towards you if you overtly show your stress, and what ways of managing that stress vis-à-vis your relationships have worked best in the past.

You may remember that when things get heated in your family, your father drinks and downloads on your mother what he really thinks and feels. Your mom remains passive, tends to panic a bit, but generally can be very compassionate towards you. Your sister often provides great advice, but she does not always respect your space. You tend to blame yourself, be anxious before a big event, but you are fine once the moment is right in front of you. You also know that you hold your stress in your body, and exercise really helps you work out the tension. You also really get a lot out of talking to your best friend. Talking to your friends helps you gain perspective and inhibits your tendency to blame yourself first when things going wrong.

Just answering these questions is a mini-therapy session in itself. The process reveals a ton of details from the past, useful information to be applied in the moment, and the power to use this knowledge in the future.

2. Change yourself to change your family

We often wish we could just fix things in other people, especially our own families. After all, we are all perfect of course! But in all seriousness, the person you can change is yourself, as it is the most effective way to have an impact on your family patterns and dynamics. Just like in physics, when one person changes, the rest of the group is forced to change and adapt.

If you find yourself shutting down every time your sister gets stressed about the bachelorette party and the bridesmaid dresses, try something new. Instead of not calling her back for days, send her an email letting her know how thankful you are that she is planning the bachelorette and recognizing how hard it has been for you to pick out a bridesmaid dress that is going to please everyone. Give her some options to unload her stress. Let her know that if she feels like the stress of planning the bachelorette is too much for her, your friend, Laura, has offered to help. And if she has mixed feelings about the bridesmaid's dress, you would welcome an open dialogue about her thoughts. You have changed your behavior, and it is inevitable that your sister will have to change hers as a result.

As Gandhi said, *"Be the change you want to see in the world."* Or in this case *"Be the change you want to see in your family."*

THE 3ʀᴅ F—FRIENDS

We've tackled the first two F's, and now we move onto the tame or tumultuous, depending on your perspective, topic of friends. Given that you are navigating new terrain as a bride, a feeling of connection and support from your friends during this time is incredibly valuable. For some brides, friends play a minor role, serving more as a backdrop of support rather than the forefront of the fanfare. For other brides, friends are a double-edged sword—an indispensable source of assurance but also a choir of constant chatter and unsolicited advice. However some brides, feel like their friends provide great solace and support.

Just as with your fiancé and your family, weddings have the potential to bring out both the good and the bad within your friendships. It is a time in life when you perhaps discover the strength of your support network and feel overwhelmed by the amount of care you receive. Or it can be a time when you feel isolated, disappointed at how few people actually "show up" for you, both literally and emotionally.

But it is important to remember that *you do have control* over this friend arena—not only over *who* you let in but also *how* you react. You are the sailor of this wedding ship, and your task is to decide who to include as your crew. You can sail this ship with just your fiancé and your family if that feels best. Or you can choose to let your friends also prop you up. You are the captain.

Triage

Your wedding is certainly not an emergency, but the crisis aspect of triage appropriately conveys the idea of first identifying those friends who are most valuable to you. To what degree you want your various friends to be part of your wedding process is not only reflective of your crisis management strategy but also *your choice* of you want to be by your side. You can let everyone in or you can choose to go it solo; you can solicit everyone's advice or call on a few key confidants along the way.

Either way, you are wise to be mindful of what type of friends you invite into your inner circle. In general, you are best served by keeping your wedding network to just a few solid, supportive, and predictable friends. While this sorting may seem calculated, it is important, as it is so easy to let a grouchy or insensitive friend negatively impact your experience. Know yourself and do what works for you. There is no perfect formula, but consciously triaging allows you to surround yourself with people who want the best for you.

Setting Reasonable Expectations

Significant life events prompt us to realign our expectations of ourselves and those around us. Given how important certain events feel to us, we reasonably expect and want people to rise to the occasion. Weddings of course are no exception to this. However, in order to stay true to the Bridal Buddha in you, it is absolutely essential to have realistic expectations for yourself and those around you. By doing as much, you will extinguish that temptation to control and ease any potential disappointment that may arise.

If you know that your fiancé's best man tends to drink too much at parties, do not expect otherwise. The best you can hope for is that he will keep his jokes clean, and while he may proceed to drink to excess, he is simply making a mockery of himself and no one else. His embarrassing behavior is not a refection of you but of him. While it is tough to stomach the thought of your proper grandmother enduring his potty-mouth, if you have decided to invite him, then you are inviting all of him—the good, the bad, the ugly. *You cannot control him or anyone else, but you can control your experience of your engagement and your wedding by setting realistic expectations.*

It may feel worthwhile to do a relationship inventory of your friends, laying out for each what you can reasonably expect from them. Look to history to be your informing guide. Do not fall prey to false hope that your "frienemy" will stop her catty jealousy. Do not set yourself up to be disappointed, thinking that your old college friend will finally emerge from isolation and be an integral part of your wedding.

✧ ✧ ✧

After careful deliberation, Sarah invited her old college roommate Bianca to be in her wedding party. Sarah went in, eyes wide open, knowing that if she asked Bianca to be a part of her wedding, then she got all of Bianca—the good, the bad and especially the wild. Her personal mantra became *"I invited her, so I get all of her."* The mantra came in handy so many times during her engagement and particularly during her wedding. Bianca was a fun-loving, loyal friend who enjoyed pushing the boundaries of fun. As sorority sisters, Sarah and Bianca have an arsenal of memories from crazy, knock-down-drunk parties during college.

However, years later, Bianca still seemed to party as if she had never graduated.

Bianca's old antics were on full display at the bachelorette party. First, Bianca offered drugs to everyone. Sarah felt totally uncomfortable and politely changed the subject. Bianca then managed to get the guy she was dating to take a picture of his penis and text it to Sarah's phone as a "fun" bachelorette party joke. This picture resurfaced the next day and caused her fiancé to ask a lot of questions.

After the bachelorette party, Sarah found herself wanting to restrict Bianca from making a toast at the rehearsal dinner, not to mention severely limiting her overall alcohol consumption. However, Sarah kept her mantra up, *"I invited her so I get all of her."* Each time she said it, it helped her let go. Sarah did not approve of Bianca's wild behavior, and yet she sincerely wanted to accept her for who she is.

In the end, Bianca surprised Sarah. At the rehearsal dinner, she gave an extremely heartfelt (and sober) toast. And at the wedding, Bianca was a necessary energy boost for a rather drab band, managing to get even Sarah's grandfather out on the dance floor. Everyone had a blast dancing the night away. Bianca livened up the celebration more than Sarah could have ever hoped for. Now, years after the wedding, Sarah finds Bianca's wild stunts to be some of the most memorable moments of her wedding.

☼   ☼   ☼

The lesson to take away—expect the same from your friends during your engagement and wedding as you would expect of them on any given day—or better yet, expect *even less* and you will find yourself pleasantly surprised.

Count Your Blessings—Feeling Fortunate for Those That "Show Up"

When the pressure is on, it is easy for a bride to get trapped in a negative thought cycle, continuously disappointed by what is not going right or who is not showing up. But it is crucial to find that antidote to disappointment and focus on those people who are indeed showing up for you in every sense of the word.

Let's take the example of Emily. The planning task had been left up to Emily entirely, and things were not going well. Emily was feeling overwhelmed and stressed. Her mom and sister had not been helpful and her fiancé had mostly taken refuge in his work. Moreover, Emily didn't have many friends on which she could rely, as her maid-of-honor had been confusingly flaky and her two other best friends had newborns at home. As her wedding date approached, Emily fixated on how her best friends had not been more supportive.

But as fate would have it, there was no room for Emily to be consumed by her disappointment when the challenges of her wedding were ultimately revealed. Emily and her fiancé were getting married in New Orleans and they arrived in the midst of a huge storm. In the next few days, as she struggled with the last-minute wedding details, it became clear that the storm was actually Hurricane Katrina. The city's levees broke and 85% of the city was flooded. There was no way most of her guests could fly in, and the wedding church and reception site were completely flooded. Suddenly all of the wedding stress and struggle were totally insignificant in the face of the natural disaster.

Fortunately their hotel was not flooded, and while Emily did not have the fancy dress, cake, or reception, she was filled with appreciation for the things that did matter. She was safe, and so were her fiancé, her mom, her sister and a handful of their closest friends. They got married by candlelight in the lobby of the hotel, with the few friends and family members who had made it to New Orleans. Everyone in the room was filled with good fortune, especially Emily, who felt overwhelmed with gratitude for those few who did consistently show up for her.

While Emily's story is extreme, it is a good reminder of the power of gratitude. Sadly, the details of a wedding can overwhelm a bride so much that all perspective is lost. If you are focused on what is going wrong, you will totally miss out on what is going right. In any given moment, take a minute to focus on the things you are grateful for, no matter how insignificant: hot water, your dress making it to the hotel, the thoughtful friend who sent you a good-luck email, your morning latte, your fiancé making you laugh. Watch your mood lift as you count your blessings.

"Gratitude is such a bulky emotion. If you let yourself REALLY feel it, it pushes everything else away."
—John O Donohue

THE FIX—FINDING EMPATHY

We have peppered this chapter with strategies and advice, ideas and directives, all in an effort to help you best manage your relationships during your engagement. But if there is one tactic that can be used above all else to help you find the quiet calm within, it is empathy.

We often get trapped in our own worlds, within our little heads, this tendency aggravated by the inherently narcissistic aspect of a wedding. Your internal world consists of your experiences, perspectives, and family history, all of which manifest in your thoughts and feelings. It is that voice that talks to you day and night. Sometimes your internal world seems like the view everyone must see, even though you intellectually know that is not true. The monumental nature of a wedding and its ostensible purpose of simply celebrating YOU is particularly reinforcing of this inability to see beyond your own lens.

But it is hard to see beyond your own perspective when your loved ones are hurting you, irritating you, or just being plain rude. When you feel slighted, it is easy to want to externalize it, lash out at the offenders, and ultimately personalize it. Your feelings may be legitimate, but that doesn't make them go away. You can end up harboring so much resentment that your wedding process gets overtaken by this rage.

Whether your interpersonal challenges are benign or major sources of stress, the fix can be the same. Take a leap and enter into your loved ones' inner worlds. Follow their emotions. Hear beyond the words they are saying. Actively understand their needs and desires. Essentially, find compassion for their perspectives.

This process of shifting your perspective to another person's internal world and finding empathy for their mindset can diffuse so many of the interpersonal conflicts that may arise while planning your wedding. It can educate you about why certain comments were made, why your sister did not show up for you, why your fiancé acted in a particular way. It can turn your feelings of hurt, anger, and frustration into understanding and compassion.

Imagine being able to step outside yourself during your engagement and step into your mother's heart, your friend's mind, and your father's role. Your mother is experiencing the child she gave birth to now devoting her life to another person. Your best friend is starting to understand that your "go-to" person is now your fiancé and not her. Your father is welcoming a new family member and realizing he is no longer the most important man in your life. These are big changes for them to process, and changes that deserve some empathy.

Engrossing yourself in alternative perspectives and feelings can be an enlightening transformation of your aggravation. It can shed light on your own shortcomings, soften your bitterness, and oftentimes act as a welcome and much-needed slice of humble pie. And ultimately, it allows you to find compassion—which in the end is all anyone really desires.

Carving out the mental space for empathy can be challenging for brides because it involves time, something that no doubt is in short supply for you right now. But by doing as much upfront, it will likely save you time—and grief—in the end. You may not agree with the perspectives of your three F's, but you can certainly make a noble effort to try to understand them.

Chapter Five
Your (Un)-dentity: Uncovering, Understanding, & Ultimately Unveiling You

---

CHAPTER CONTENTS:

Uncovering: Peeling Back the Core of the Cake

The Quintessential Case—Ashley's Story
Primary vs. Secondary Emotions
Who Am I?
But I Don't Deserve This
Where Did "Me" Go?

Understanding: The Impact of the Past on Your Wedding

New Life, Old Patterns
New Future, Old Scars

Unveiling You & Your Worth

Old Friend—Self Doubt; New Friend—Self Worth

In the west, we are goal oriented. We know where we want to go, and we are very directed in getting there. This may be useful, but often we forget to enjoy ourselves along the route. There is a word in Buddhism that means "wishlessness" or "aimlessness." The idea is that you do not put something in front of you and run after it because everything is already here, in yourself.

Thich Nhat Hanh—*Peace is in Every Step*

UNCOVER: PEELING BACK
THE CORE OF THE CAKE

You may opt for a cake with layer after layer of chocolate goodness. Your dress may have tier after tier of fabric. And your homemade invitation may be multi-layered so as to incorporate all of the travel information for your destination wedding.

Just as these tangibles of a wedding are multi-dimensional, so too is what this whole process signifies when it comes to your identity and sense of self. On the surface, your wedding may simply represent a celebration of your relationship, but deep inside it feels like a transformation of self. Superficially, this wedding is about you, but beyond that posturing, you feel uncomfortable putting so much emphasis on yourself.

Rite-of-passage experiences and the subsequent emotional reactions they produce are often multi-layered. What appears on the surface is not the entirety of the story; instead it is more dynamic and complicated and rich in meaning.

This chapter is about peeling back the layers of your wedding process and uncovering what else is going on inside of you. What exists below that surface-level reaction or emotion? What does this all say about your perceived identity and level of self-worth? Why does something as ostensibly superficial as a wedding bring up something as deeply painful as a past experience?

These are deliberately vague questions, but dynamic ones nonetheless, which allow room for your own meaning to make its way to the surface and for you to garner a deeper understanding of your sense of self as it relates to your wedding.

The Quintessential Case—Ashley's Story

After a memorable and meaningful proposal, Ashley tiptoed into the planning process, choosing to savor the residual feelings of excitement from her engagement rather than diving face-first into the wedding. She deliberately took her time in deciding the when, where, and how, but after a few months of pondering, it became clear that she was stuck in indecisiveness.

Ashley was torn on whether to get married in her small hometown in Ohio or at a Mexican resort, a seemingly stark choice but one that was complicated by deeper issues. She wanted to honor her roots, but she also wanted to make a statement about her new worldliness. She desired to show her appreciation for her mom raising her single-handedly in this Midwest community. However, by having the wedding there, Ashley feared it would feel isolating and rejecting for her father. And while she had dreamed about a beach wedding since starting to date Michael, she felt conflicted about pulling the trigger. It was an extravagance for which she ultimately felt unworthy given all the financial struggles she and her single mom had endured during her childhood. Ashley's father was finally stepping up to the plate and paying for the wedding, and while she wanted to feel grateful, instead her resentments about his lack of support in the past festered and complicated this decision.

As Ashley's experience so clearly exemplifies, planning is rife with multi-layered meaning. It is not just about hometown versus beach, but a feeling of choosing mom versus dad. Ashey's choice was not just frugality versus extravagance, but her comfort with self-sacrifice versus her evolving sense of self-worth. What a wedding brings up for brides is complicated, rich in family history, and deserving of understanding so that you can walk away from this experience with a deeper sense of self.

Primary vs. Secondary Emotions

A first step in this process towards self-exploration is becoming acquainted with the concept of primary and secondary emotions. The concepts are not complicated but the meaning they may unveil can be.

The primary emotion with which you have become so familiar during your engagement may be masking the secondary emotion that holds a deeper meaning. In life, as with your engagement, there are probably one or two emotions that you re-use again and again, essentially your *go-to emotions*. These are the emotions that you feel the safest expressing, automatically falling into them most often, or the most acceptable in your family-of-origin. These are your *primary emotions*. Perhaps you find yourself frequently impatient or angry, or maybe you fall back on feelings of stress, insecurity, or confusion.

A key piece of taking inventory in these moments is to ask yourself what else is going on inside. When you peel off the first layer of anger or stress or insecurity, what other feelings do you find? These underlying emotions may feel more intense, painful, or scary to acknowledge. The interior emotions may inspire guilt and shame, calling up experiences from your past. They may be the ones you believe to be socially unacceptable for your gender, family, class, or race. These are your *secondary* emotions.

Oftentimes we dismiss these core emotions because we gravitate to our go-to emotions so easily, stopping there and failing to take inventory of the emotions that are more difficult to acknowledge and accept. But these core secondary emotions are rich in information that can greatly help you understand your choices and any difficulties with which you may be grappling.

Let's say you are upset and pissed at your photographer's unwillingness to take time to plan out a photo agenda, thus inviting you to "flame mail" him. But if you took some time to uncover what is underneath, you may find feelings of abandonment and disconnection—yet another person is letting you down and you are not sure who to ask for support. Yes, you are angry but, more importantly, you are also feeling isolated and alone. With this deeper level of understanding, you are able to tend to those "wounds." Perhaps finding a person you can confide in (whether it is a friend, your fiancé, or a counselor) would be helpful to start understanding the underlying emotions. Even picking up a journal to write down some of these deeper thoughts and feelings can feel incredibly revealing and supportive.

Let's try on another example. You are feeling unbelievably stressed about your wedding dress: it just isn't looking as you imagined it would. At your first fitting, you asked the seamstress to take out a few layers of tulle in the skirt. But at your second fitting, the dress still feels really puffy around the butt. You ask again, but this time the dressmaker protests and throws up her hands. On the surface you are *stressed*. You take pride in being the *good client* who never causes too much fuss, but you saved up for this dress for over a year and you want it to look right.

But as you take a moment to check in with yourself, you realize you are also feeling *angry and hurt.* You pick up your phone and call your maid-of-honor. By unloading, you "own" not only your feeling of stress but also your feelings of anger and hurt—after all, your seamstress did not listen to you at the last fitting. Your maid-of-honor confirms you have every right to be upset and then encourages you to ask for what you need and want (even if it means causing a fuss!). *"You only get married once. Just keep asking for what you want until they do it. Who cares if you have to get a million fittings?"* You take a deep breath and feel yourself cooling off. She is right. Your wedding is months away and you can just keep on coming back.

Recognizing a primary emotion versus a secondary emotion is a huge component to understanding the complexity of your emotional world during your wedding. Rather than feeling helpless and confused by your primary emotion, find clarity and solace in your secondary one. This process of discernment is enlightening and will ultimately make you feel more in control of your emotions.

Who Am I?

Okay, we admit that this is a ridiculously big question. It may even seem silly to ask at this point in your life. However, it is a very important question as you make the transition from "single hottie" to bride and then finally to wife.

Getting married invites many potential changes in your life: sharing money and a home with your fiancé, changing your name, splitting holidays and vacations with a new family, cementing your own family unit (you and your husband) separate from your own parents and siblings, and vowing to be a loyal and devoted wife. In the face of these changes, how do you see yourself and what actions do you feel compelled to make?

Some brides feel strange about being financially tied to someone and start to feel resentful when household duties of laundry and cleaning start to pile up. Many women lose sleep (understandably) over losing their last name. Some are heartbroken when they have to choose between cooking Thanksgiving dinner with their family or their fiancé's. Many brides feel like they no longer get invited out for cocktails by their single girlfriends, even though they are longing for the female bonding. Some brides feel they should de-friend their ex-boyfriends on Facebook, even though that statement seems a bit silly. Some brides feel torn between being true and loyal to their parents, to their fiancé, or to themselves.

During this time, when your identity is undergoing a massive transformation, it is easy to lose track of who you are and what you want. The following stories of Laura, Desiree, and Lisa portray brides who had to really dive in deep and ask themselves this very important question.

Laura: At the onset of her wedding planning, Laura was fortunate enough to further discover who she really is and what she really values in relation to her mom, although this revelation came via some uncomfortable tension between her and her mother. Laura's mom was dead-set on a large social wedding at her brother's estate, a venue that could accommodate up to 350 guests.

Laura had made her parents proud her whole life, a trait she took pride in. She was a daughter who loved to please. However, as soon as the unthinkable 350 number escaped her mother's lips, Laura knew this was not what she wanted. In her early 20s, she would have just said, "*Mom, whatever makes you happy.*" But the wiser bride-to-be knew she had to delicately say no and bare the brunt of her mom's disappointment. Laura was not just her mother's daughter. She was her own person, a woman who was able to express her opinions and needs. And that clarity on who she is and what she wants informed her that a large wedding would simply be too much pressure for her. Laura had never been as extroverted as her mother, and for the first time in her life, she did not feel ashamed or guilty about this truth.

Desiree: One day while snowboarding with a friend, Desiree found herself contemplating "who she is." In between runs, she took a reflective break on a hill overlooking the mountain range. Her friend Leah came over and asked what was on her mind. Desiree told her that although she really wanted to take her fiancé's last name, suddenly it all just seemed very strange, almost unreal. Being an athlete and part of countless sports teams, people had always called Desiree by her last name—"Smithy." Desiree told her friend, "*I don't mind giving up my last name for a family name we share, but Jasperson is going to take a while to feel like me.*" Leah listened and reminded her that "*change can be challenging even if you know it is what you want.*" While names are ostensibly just labels, they are an integral part of one's identity; thus, Desiree's discomfort with such a change makes perfect sense.

Lisa: The morning after Lisa got engaged, she admitted to herself that she really did not like her ring. It was sparkly and gorgeous, but the setting was too delicate for her fingers. Even though her opinion was genuine, she felt so shallow and superficial for not loving the ring. Lisa's internal voice kept circling the same thoughts, *"Who the hell am I to not be grateful for a present that cost thousands of dollars and that is supposed to be about love? Who have I become to even care about such a thing? What kind of wife am I going to make with this kind of attitude?"*

As much as Lisa was thrilled to spend the rest of her life with her husband-to-be, she felt the engagement ring was just not reflective of her. She decided that she would try it out for two weeks, and if it still felt strange, she would let her fiancé know. Two weeks passed and Lisa still hated the ring. She had promised herself that she would say something at this point, although she was utterly scared and felt superficial. She wanted to be the "good wife" who graciously accepted her husband's gifts. But she also suddenly realized that a "good wife" was one who was honest with her feelings. Plus, Lisa knew that her fiancé ultimately wanted her to be happy. On a walk after dinner, Lisa took a deep breath and broached the subject, *"Larry, please do not take this the wrong way. I am so sure about how good we are as a couple, about you, and about our wedding, but I am not sure I love this ring setting."* She held out her ring, and felt a wave of relief when Larry responded, *"I did my best, but there were so many options, and I wanted to surprise you. Let's find you a setting you LOVE. Hopefully, you are going to be wearing that thing for the rest of your life. You better like it!"*

But I Don't Deserve This...

A wedding shower is arguably an awkward event. It is meant to be an opportunity for your friends and family to shower you with love and support, but it fairly can be deemed an odd tradition, full of uncomfortable moments as you rip through a pile of gifts while everyone watches. *"Oh, a fondue set. I have always wanted one of these,"* even though you have a couple of unopened ones at home. You may even feel fake as you try your best to act surprised and grateful. Even if you are totally extroverted, you may have a hard time taking in all the attention, gifts, and celebration. You may feel totally strange and find yourself wondering, *"How could little me be worthy of this much attention?"*

While engagement parties and showers are meant to be fun and fantastic, they often end up feeling more materialistic than meaningful. However, these celebrations are *tremendously significant rituals that prepare for your wedding.* They are representative of the network that has come together to support you as you enter this next phase of your life together.

Look around at these pre-wedding parties and take objective notes. A shower or an engagement party is a mini-version of your wedding day. These are the people who are here to support you in good times and in bad as you become husband and wife. Try to put aside the discomfort and take in the warm wishes, the gifts, and the love. You deserve to feel celebrated during this special time in life. Everyone does.

Where Did "Me" Go?

Ann remembers totally losing herself in the wedding process. She knew she was in trouble when she started ditching her weekly one-on-ones with her boss to attend dress fittings, and when she couldn't stop surfing the wedding blogs instead of making her deadlines. She had worked for years to land the job of her dreams in a fabulous design firm and now she was throwing it away for a white dress and a big party. Ann tried to get back on track at work, but she felt out of control and obsessed with the details of her wedding. When she was single, she would tease her engaged friends for "freaking out" about their weddings, and now she was the one who could not shut up about it.

Ann rationalized her wedding obsessiveness as harmless until she was so busy burning wedding CDs that she forgot her maid-of-honor's birthday. This was her best friend and someone who had been extremely supportive of her over the past six months, and her whole life for that matter. Ann was known to be a loyal friend, who often baked her friends cookies and organized birthday celebrations, but now she was the selfish bride who was spacing on anything not related to her wedding day. She was shocked and embarrassed. Not only was she being a flake at work (after clawing her way to the top), but now she was also letting her best friend down. But yet it continued, as the next day Ann hung up on her little sister for complaining about a 7:00 a.m. hair appointment. Such a confrontational and unusual exchange shook Ann to the core, and she felt frightened, *what the heck has happened to me?!*

If wedding planning is beginning to feel so consuming that you are wondering where "me" went, take a step back and remember you are more than a bride. You are also a sister, a daughter, a partner, a fiancée, a friend, a granddaughter, an employee, and so much more. You are someone who cares about other people, has talents and interests beyond wedding planning, and has dreams other than your wedding day. Yes, this is an important rite of passage and a special day, yet you also possess many other qualities. Even though these other parts of you may not be shining as bright as your identity as a bride right now, they are still you. And once all the fanfare has died down, rest assured that you will be able to return to that side of you.

UNDERSTAND: PATTERNS OF THE PAST & THEIR IMPACT ON THE PRESENT

A tree's rings and structure provide all the information one would need to understand why it is a certain way today. There is evidence of why it leans a certain direction (to soak up the nourishing sun), why the bark is so thick (to ward off those feisty bugs), and why it has more leaves on one side than the other (that blasted wind). The tree has adapted over time to its surrounding conditions to be as strong as possible.

Like a tree, as a child you learned to adapt to your environment to survive, flourish, and grow. You instinctively found ways to get nourishment under the different conditions that your childhood presented to you, and you developed a belief system that enabled you to mesh with the various environments you confronted.

But just as the tree grows stronger as it ages, so

too do you. You are no longer a dependent girl reliant on your family for nourishment—you are self-sufficient and have control over your environment. And just as the tree adapts over time to any environmental changes, so does your belief system, particularly when you reach adulthood and find yourself in new terrain, such as planning your wedding.

New Life, Old Patterns

Even though you have arguably "launched" from the familial nest, during your engagement you may feel like you are back in old conditions. It perhaps feels similar to when you first traveled home to your parents' house as an adult. You returned to your childhood room, heated family dinners and your mom's endless advice, and you started to feel like a child all over again. Old feelings and patterns reemerged; time had seemingly stood still, and it felt as if you had never left home.

This same sensation can be activated by your wedding. It's like shopping for your prom dress with your mother all over again. Even if you are planning and paying for your wedding entirely on your own, your family will still likely rear its head and reactivate those old family patterns. While some patterns may feel nicely familiar and reassuring, others may drive you nuts and make it particularly hard for you to find a voice. You have changed, but your family system has not. Your belief system has evolved over the years, but your family's has likely remained the same. You have new ideas for how life (and weddings!) can look, but your parents do not.

Instead, you find yourself recycling old patterns

and reliving old dynamics, all while trying to plan a wedding. Rather than celebrating your love for your fiancé, you feel instantly insecure about affectionately touching him at your parent's home, recoiling at your mother's directive to stay pure. You feel self-consciously adolescent in the face of your grandmother's constant banter about your weight and choice of wedding attire. You easily fall back into your family role of peacemaker, mediating between the strong-headed opinions of your mother and your sister. It's all enough to make you want to elope.

When you start planning your wedding, *in many ways you are emotionally traveling home to visit with your family.* It may feel as if you are visiting your parents' home as well as your fiancé's home for 14 months in a row. This is particularly tricky, because both you and your fiancé are trying to adapt to your old environments while also forging your new identity as a couple.

Given its prevalence for brides, this return to the old family patterns is almost a miniature rite of passage in itself. Yet, you are no longer that little girl having to adapt. You are an adult now and have the power to cultivate your own environment and encourage new family behaviors and patterns that respect and reflect your new role as an individuated woman.

You may have felt controlled by your mother as a child, and as you plan your wedding, you may again feel like your mother is trying to control you. Even though you intellectually wonder whose wedding this is—hers or mine—inside you feel that you must conform and follow your mother's directions. You have activated an old family pattern of adaptation and appeasement, and you may not have even realized that you are doing it. It is second nature because you have done this your whole life in order to survive.

Yet, if you take the time to step back, look at this old pattern, and *think* about its ramifications, you may realize you do not have to do it her way. You may *feel* like you do, but your intellectual and rational side informs you that you do not. If your father retreats to his withdrawn side, you no longer have to try to engage him in conversations about the wedding unless you really want to. If you have been raised to portray a certain family image, as an adult you have the choice to serve hot dogs even if your family thinks it is not proper. If you feel like you must honor your family's religious practices, this is a choice that you alone can make. You no longer have to adapt to your family unless you want to. You have differentiated yourself with your own belief system, and your voice is louder and more powerful than the little girl you once were.

If you only take one thing from this chapter, *remember you are now an adult. You no longer have to adapt to your environment. You have the ability and power to create new family patterns that respect your individuality.*

New Future, Old Scars—Repairing Wounding for Future Strength

Sometimes when we look at a tree we can see that someone has carved his or her initials into it. This may remain a wound in the tree, which the bark can never completely cover. This deep marking remains a characteristic of the tree. It is an etched reminder of the past, for everyone to see and the tree to feel.

During your engagement, your unhealed scabs and wounds may be scratched and picked at, igniting some emotional pain. Weddings, with their multidimensional significance, have the power to recall painful events from the past, even if they aren't ostensibly related. This is particularly true with deaths and important relationship losses. If your father passed away many years ago, your engagement may be a time you miss him even more. You may wish he could be there to meet your future husband, provide you with some fatherly advice, or walk you down the aisle. Even though you have missed your father every day since his passing, the longing now may feel that much more acute. You crave his attention and his calm presence. You wish he could show his savvy dance steps and wow the guests with a sentimental father-of-the-bride speech. Your loss feels magnified and different than before, since there is now a new context in which you miss your father.

Or perhaps you were the youngest in your family. By the time you were old enough to drive, to leave home, or to drink, no one cared. All of your clothes were hand-me-downs, and you were always living in the shadow of your siblings. Your wedding feels no different. Although you spent years of your life traveling to your siblings' weddings and baby showers, your wedding is being treated like a non-event.

Or perhaps your parents worked full-time and you never felt like you got enough help or guidance as a child. And now, as a bride, the same sort of awful feelings emerge when your groom works late every night and is unable to help with any sort of wedding planning. Or maybe as a child you felt tortured by a queen bee bully, never sure if you fit in with your classmates. And now, as a bride, you take every decline RSVP personally, feeling unpopular and unliked because your groom has more friends coming than you do. You are reminded of all those difficult, left-out feelings. And sometimes these wounds of the past can feel doubly painful in the present.

✧ ✧ ✧

Lucy's story is an example of an old childhood pattern that was rekindled during the wedding process. Lucy had never felt emotionally supported by her mom, who was too preoccupied with her own anxiety and life "dramas." In turn, Lucy had become a very independent and self-sufficient young woman, who left home early, found a group of very close and supportive friends, and worked her way through college and graduate school.

However, she always hoped things would change with her mother. She rationally believed that with time, her mother would no longer be so preoccupied with herself and absent from Lucy's life. Unfortunately, Lucy's theory did not hold up; her mother's behavior throughout the wedding process was just as preoccupied and absent as she always had been. And each time Lucy's mother let her down, it felt incredibly (and familiarly) painful. It not only hurt in the moment but reminded her of all the times in the past that her mom had flaked, failed to call her back, or was unable to support her.

Lucy had to face the fact that her relationship with her mom was not going to change before her wedding, and perhaps not ever. Lucy reminded herself of the courage it took to leave home and how hard she had worked to put herself through college; she did not want to regress now. Lucy replaced her need for support from her mother by turning to her bridesmaids—the same group of amazing women she had found when she left home. Although her friends were no substitute for what a mom represents, they were able to celebrate and support her during this very special time. That in itself was a huge gift.

✧　✧　✧

As painful as it may be, your wedding affords you the opportunity to reflect on your wounds. It is a rare chance to massage them, tend to them, and ultimately heal them to the degree they can be healed. Sit with the feelings that come up. Talk to someone who feels safe. Meditate on your thoughts. Untie those knots within you. Build your bark. This is a chance to grow from the past and transition into the next phase of your life a stronger woman.

UNVEILING YOU & YOUR WORTH

Weddings are such new terrain for most brides that it is almost inevitable to feel pangs of self-doubt as you try to figure out the planning madness. After all, there were no college courses on how to craft a wedding, nor did your mom ever model much in the form of party planning. Given that you may feel a bit lost about the task ahead, it is pretty easy to fall prey to self-doubt—either in new disguise or in the old, familiar form.

You have so many decisions to make, so many relationships to manage, and an emotional transition to marriage to manage. It's a lot to hold on your plate at one time, and you may feel like you just don't know what you are doing. This first tier of self-doubt around planning is natural. But left to its own devices, it can be potentially dangerous, as it can open the door to old insecurities from your past and elicit more self-battery.

Let's be clear: your challenge in planning a wedding is great, especially in the face of considerable obstacles, such as family dynamics and old insecurities. But you can do everything in your power to use your wedding as a building block towards an increased level of self-worth and self-love.

Your Old Friend—Self Doubt; Your New Friend—Self Worth

You are enough just as you are.

HAH, you say. *It certainly doesn't feel that way.* Instead you have mixed feelings about your own self-concept and doubt if you really are enough just as you are, especially in the face of a wedding!

Do any of these voices from inside your head sound familiar?

- *If I lost 10 more pounds, I would be so much better.*
- *I am such an idiot for saying such a thing to my mother-in-law.*
- *I am a bad daughter for not being able to please my mom.*
- *My wedding is going to be boring, just like me.*

Wow! That is really harsh self-talk. While it is unrealistic to ask you to immediately throw that negativity out the church door, you may want to try to offset it with at least the same amount of positive internal dialogue.

Find Your Inner Superhero

Essentially, you want to combat your faulty negative thinking by spending ample time appreciating yourself and your strengths. Create a mental list of the qualities that you *love about yourself.* Do you love the way you can laugh at yourself? Do you love your loyalty to your friends? Do you love your ability to listen to your fiancé? Do you love your calm demeanor? Are you a talented cook? Are you good at your job?

Make this list long and detailed. Use the list as your mental tape recorder. Allow it to play back these attributes to you, because they *are* you. We often focus on our deficits but do not always take the time to remind ourselves of our strengths. You *can* control your own negative self-talk and judgments; it just takes conscious effort and a bit of determination.

Another angle on replacing the negativity with positivism is to try to see at least two lenses of yourself. View what's going on in both the yin and the yang, the feminine and the masculine. If you are feeling like you are leaving a lot of people off your guest list, think of all the people you are including. When you try on dresses and lament your freckly skin, focus on what you do like, your defined shoulders. If you feel shame for having gone way over budget, find pride in the fact that you have been honest about it to your family and fiancé.

This is not about being a super-bubbly cheerleader

in every moment or a dramatic "emo" girl. Instead it is about gathering evidence to support a more healthy way of thinking and feeling. If a situation feels negative and one-sided, dig until you find the other side to view it from. Use your creativity and give yourself a break by adopting a more loving reaction to *you.*

Altar of Inspiration

Harsh self-talk can dramatically interfere with your engagement and end up making the whole experience a huge downer—you obviously don't want to go that route. You need to combat that voice of self-doubt. Another way to consciously comfort your inner worrier is to create a visual reminder of all the wonderful things that inspire you.

One study found that the biggest indicator of work happiness is the number of pictures people had on their desks. These researchers hypothesized that being surrounded by pictures of loved ones enhanced a worker's job satisfaction and quality of life. It makes sense—a glance at the picture of a loved one invites feelings of gratitude and gives you a momentary mental break from any daily hassles.

An *altar of inspiration* is a dedicated space, typically in your home, to display a collection of items, images, keepsakes or objects that are significant to you in some way. The space can be a bulletin board, a special drawer in your desk, a small corner of your garden or deck, or even a box. What matters is that it accommodates those things that are inspiring and confidence-boosting for you.

As you prepare for your wedding, try to notice the

149

meaningful symbols that emerge in your life—those things that not only inspire intense feelings of wonder, joy, or calm, but also the things that make you feel good about yourself: the ones that make you smile inside, remind you of your accomplishments, or bring a moment of serenity to your day.

Perhaps it is a shell that you brought back from your first beach vacation with your fiancé, an old card or cartoon that welcomed you to your new career, an image that represents your passion for photography, a special ribbon that commemorates your charitable spirit, a scrap of wrapping paper from the most meaningful gift you ever received, a dried flower from your graduation, or a childhood picture that captures your carefree nature. You may come across these special treasures unexpectedly in your day-to-day life—a pine cone on the pavement or a beautiful stamp on a post card—or you may already know the exact things that encourage and inspire you.

Once you have your collection, you can arrange them, collage them, or just let your items organically pile up in your space of inspiration. Notice how your dedicated space engages your senses. Take in the shapes, textures, smells, colors and the feeling of each item. Use this place as an anchor and a reminder of all the good that you contain. You are filling your wedding day with beautiful flowers, fabrics, and music; this task of collecting and creating encourages you to fill your head with beautiful things too.

Uncover, Understand, Unveil

Getting engaged can rock your world as well as your identity. Some of the most interesting and competent brides find this the most challenging part of the wedding process. Whether it is losing yourself with wedding planning, getting caught up in old family dynamics, or your struggle over whether to change your name, it all happens to the strongest of women. Yet, those who take the opportunity to journey within themselves seem to emerge with even more depth and complexity.

Ostensibly your engagement is about honoring your love towards your fiancé. Yet this is also a time to honor your own self. So many loved ones are coming forward to celebrate you, and you need to join in the choir of their praise. You are worthy of the attention. You have a world of strengths within you, and those who love you know as much. Find a way to truly believe that you are beautiful just the way you are.

Chapter Six
The Finale—Supporting Yourself on the Big Day

CHAPTER CONTENTS:

Your Emotional Game Plan
(Pre) Wedding "Video"
The 3-Step "Quickie" Calmer
Body Building

Bad Behaviors – How to Manage the Rude, the Ridiculous, & the Absurd

Your Metaphorical Anchor

You have made it. You have transcended the stress and the superficiality and have planned a wedding that is reflective of you. You have successfully managed your parents, your friends, and your fiancé—the process surprisingly even allowing for a deeper level of closeness. And you feel as confident as you have been in a long while, having finally settled into what it means to be a bride and secure in what it means to be a wife.

You have survived the planning game. And now you need to survive—and flourish—on game day.

If you are like other brides, you probably have spent countless hours thinking about your dress, your reception, the clever invitations, and on and on, but you may have not spent much time thinking about *how* you want to experience your wedding day. Who has the time to think about this, right? And yet, how you experience your wedding day is very important.

Jessica's story is about what not to do on the day of your wedding. Her parents were upset that she was getting married so young and marrying someone so old; she was 19 and he was 39. Consequently, during her engagement, Jessica never spoke to her parents and isolated herself from her friends. On the day of her wedding, she saw all of her girlfriends in their purple bridesmaid dresses for the first time. The girls had tried to warn Jessica about how awful the back looked, but she had ignored their concerns. Jessica's jaw dropped when she saw just how backless the dresses were, dipping well below the waist line. Plus, all of her girlfriends were from her running club and had drastic sportsbra tans. "*Oh no you are all going to be facing the back of the church with these low-cut dresses and zebra looking backs!* " Things continued to veer from what she had planned—the photographer was late and her flowers were covered in an ugly netting. Having isolated herself so much during the engagement, Jessica didn't know who to turn to for support. The wedding day spiraled out of control and she was never able to calm herself down. Her father basically carried her down the aisle and she was an absent zombie during the reception.

Meghan, on the other hand, is a bride who mentally and emotionally grew stronger through her engagement so that she had the fortitude to turn her wedding day around. The day started off with an energizing run on the beach. It was an absolutely gorgeous day, and Meghan's mood was good. However, hours later, her nerves set in and her mood tanked after a rude (and loud) comment from her maid-of-honor about how the custom-made bridal hair piece kept falling out. Then her gown was accidentally torn before the ceremony, and her photographer was a complete no-show. Her wedding high had transformed into a wedding low. The best man tried to call the photographer, only to find out that he had double-booked and was "running late." Crap! Her day was not turning out how she had envisioned.

Meghan made a game-time decision to move pictures to after the ceremony and extend the cocktail hour for the guests. She was totally frustrated by the photographer's lack of professionalism but was relieved to have some extra time to fix her hair piece and her dress. Sitting in front of the mirror, she took a deep breath and checked in with herself. She was starving, thirsty, and feeling pretty annoyed—not a great way to head down the aisle. After the hair piece and the dress were fixed, she grabbed a bottle of water, forced down a sandwich, and snuck one of her best friends to the back room of the church for a laugh session. It felt awesome to take a time-out from the rest of the wedding drama. Thirty minutes later the guests were in the church and she was walking down the aisle, feeling calm and ready to say "I do."

Now that you are ready for the finale, it is time to put the icing on the cake and come up with your game plan for ensuring optimal enjoyment on your wedding day. To draw upon another sports analogy, you are going into this game a few points down—it is extremely difficult to stay balanced and relaxed on your wedding day when you are flooded with stress hormones and adrenaline. But a well thought-out strategy can beat that stress team.

YOUR EMOTIONAL GAME PLAN

(Pre) Wedding "Video"

Spend some time imagining and visualizing your wedding day. Start from the first moment you open your eyes to your last sip of champagne before "consummating" the marriage. Think about the people with whom you want to spend your wedding day; the cast will likely vary depending on what scene you are in. While getting your hair done, you may just want your bridesmaids. When putting on your dress, perhaps you just want your mom there, as it feels like such a symbolic moment. Or perhaps there are times when you will just want to be left alone; be clear on your desires in advance and set the boundaries accordingly.

You would also be wise to envision how you want to spend your downtime during the day. Many brides have felt their stress increase if there is too much inactivity. You may want to schedule in a workout or a massage. Or perhaps you will want one last meal with just your immediate family. Be specific and concrete about what you want to do, while leaving room for potential changes. (After all, you have squashed Bridezilla for this whole process and you don't want her rigidity to emerge in the last scene!) If your wishes shift during the day and you go off-script, ask for what you need. Everyone wants to support you, but they cannot read your mind. Your support crew wants to feel useful, so put them to work.

Most brides agree that making one's wedding day as simple as possible is key. Do not overschedule, make room for the deep meaning of it all, and be true to your Bridal Buddha. After all, in the end, you want to stay consistent to the vision and temperament that you have carried throughout your planning process and parlay it into the finale.

The 3-Step "Quickie" Calmer

Let's be clear—you will not have time to dive into any deep psychological tricks on your wedding day. That's why we have come up with the 3-Step "Quickie" to calm your nerves and center you when you start to feel a bit maxed out.

(1) Come up with a theme song, ideally a song that brings you back to an empowering moment or that makes you feel good or perhaps garners a laugh. When you feel the need, play it on your iPod or hum it inside your head.

(2) Think of an image you find to be calming and inspiring. Perhaps it is standing on the edge of the ocean or looking out at the sun setting over the mountains. Or maybe it is as simple as your wedding ring.

(3) Come up with a mantra or a few words that will help you relax. *Everything will work out; I am supported and surrounded by the ones who love me; It is all good.*

When you find yourself getting lost, stressed, or pulled into some sort of drama, come back to your mantra, your theme song, or your image. Use these "quickies" to calm you, balance you, or take you to a fun place inside your head. Just a few lines of your theme song (Lady Gaga, anyone?) can completely shift your mood and get you back on track to enjoying your wedding day.

Body Building

You have probably worked exceptionally hard tending to every area of your body in preparation for your wedding—from diet to nails to skin. You are in the final stretch, but don't get lazy in this arena too soon. Given all that is going on in that final week, it is really easy to neglect your physical needs on the day of your wedding. Think through how you are going to stay nourished and hydrated that day. You may even want to have a game plan for alcohol consumption. Champagne may be abundant, but food may be scarce. One thought is to give your maid-of-honor the job of making sure you get a round of appetizers or water before your first glass of bubbly. Many brides forget to eat and forsake water, but it is virtually impossible to stay balanced and happy without any fuel.

Hopefully you will wisely realize the benefit of eating some eggs or a big bagel smothered with cream cheese at breakfast. But if you don't, at the first sign of stress (a slight headache, a stomach pain, or neck tension), take a minute to pause and check in with your body. Take a deep breath, drink a glass of water, and eat something that will sustain you through the evening. And if you have the time, why not also recite your mantra, sing your theme song, and call up that inspiring visual? Nourishing your body and your mind on the day of your wedding will greatly impact your ability to show up and enjoy it.

BAD BEHAVIOR—HOW TO MANAGE THE RUDE, RIDICULOUS, AND ABSURD

Be prepared. Someone *will be* rude, inappropriate, or outright outrageous at your wedding. It may be your aunt with her continual "*oh dear, you just got too skinny. I hardly recognize you.*" Or perhaps it is your old college friend who decides to forego the reception at the last minute; her date couldn't make it and she couldn't possibly "bear it alone." Or, of course, you may be cursed by the old stereotypical drunk who carries his antics way too far.

These scenarios may make you tense, cause your nostrils to flare in anger, or simply make you want to weep. But rest assured, with a little preparation and some thick skin, you can endure the rude, the ridiculous, and the absurd—and perhaps laugh at it along the way.

Know it is normal. You are not the first bride to be disrespected or embarrassed and you certainly won't be the last. Rudeness on your wedding day is part and parcel of the process, yet another mini rite of passage, and one that you will transition through unscathed.

Be the Princess. In the face of a ridiculous comment or situation, be true to your attire and be a lady. Pause before you say anything, breathe, take a step back, and either walk away or say something exceptionally lady-like. *It has been a pleasure talking with you, but it is time for me to make my way to the cake.* Stay poised and stay in character. You will find so much consolation after the fact in knowing you handled the situation like a true lady.

Keep a sense of humor. Tap into your funny bone and see some of these mishaps in the comical light they usually can be seen in. It may be mortifying to see your brother in tuxedo pants that are two sizes too small, but it is also darn funny. Laughter has amazing power to heal and provide perspective.

✧ ✧ ✧

Maddy maintained her composure and elegance during even the worst parts of their best man's toast. Maddy's fiancé and his best man had been the closest of friends since kindergarten. In his toast, he shared how they had dreamed they would meet and marry beautiful girls who were best friends. Yet, a seemingly benign story got really messy when the best man stated *"yeah, but we don't always end up with the women we think we will end up with when we are kids."* The disaster continued when he proceeded to call Maddy "Sarah," her fiancé's old longtime girlfriend. Maddy rolled with the punches and stayed calm. Deep down she knew what he was trying to say and that he meant well. Maddy kept her sense of humor, hugged him after the toast and calmly said into the microphone, *"Great speech, Fred."* His name was Jason.

Maddy's laidback attitude set the tone for the wedding. People relaxed and had a blast. Jason felt horrible about his toast but it was one of the great memories from their wedding. To this day, Maddy jokingly calls Jason "Fred" when he calls the house asking for her husband. Everyone laughs, remembering the fun they had at the wedding

✧ ✧ ✧

Jaime had asked her stepsister Tory, her maid-of-honor, to help with certain duties the day of her wedding. However, the plan got off-kilter when Tory started drinking that morning at a women's luncheon. When she got to the hotel suite to start with hair and makeup, Tory went on and on about how she was sore from all the oral sex she had received the night before from one of Jamie's cousins. Too much information in general, but particularly since the flower girl and mother-in-law were in the room too!

However, Jamie actually thought her maid-of-honor's behavior was really funny. Jamie knew it only reflected on Tory, and in the end it served as tension-breaking entertainment. Jamie was a good sport about Tory's antics until she started hitting on her widowed father. After the cake cutting, Jamie had to make a beeline for the bar and ask Tory to cut it out and get back on the dance floor. Yet, despite Tory's missteps, the memory of her maid-of-honor draped all over her widowed father is one of the funniest things she remembers from her wedding. Remember, time breeds perspective and unveils the humor.

✧ ✧ ✧

YOUR METAPHORICAL ANCHOR

Where in life do you really trust yourself? What is an arena that is your domain, that is devoid of self-doubt; a place where are able to be present and focus; an activity or hobby that makes you feel like you are the author or designer of your life? From this place, you

161

lead with purpose and integrity. When challenges arise or things go wrong, you call up this anchor to cope and then move on. Perhaps it is when you are hiking in the outdoors or playing the piano. Maybe you really trust yourself when you are singing, cooking, or walking. Maybe you remember how you felt when you played soccer in high school. This symbolic place is a well-spring of strength. Use this place as your core or your anchor on your wedding day—a metaphor that you can use to bring you balance, calm, and peace.

Sarah loved to sing opera. When she was on-stage, everything else dropped away and she felt present, alive, and empowered. The stage was her domain. She pictured the day of her wedding as the opera of her own creation. She was in charge. When she wanted to shift her mood and get back in balance on her wedding day, she would sing a solo in her head that would make her feel grounded. When she needed some distance from her bridesmaids and family members, she pictured herself tuning out the choir. When she needed to take a moment for herself, she pictured herself closing the curtains between acts. For Sarah, opera was her symbolic anchor. And when she "missed a note" on the day of her wedding (her priest was late and her brother's speech was a little strange), she just kept singing.

✧ ✧ ✧

Yoga is also a powerful metaphor for many women. The practice of hatha yoga brings about emotional stability and clarity of mind. Applying the principles of yoga to your wedding day can be the exact antidote you need to quell all that is going on around you. Yoga teachers will often refer to "your practice": that which is only yours and true for you in the moment. In yoga class, when you are feeling unbalanced and emotionally unclear, your teacher may encourage you to tap into the inner calm that is inside of you.

On the day of your wedding, if you begin to feel overwhelmed, think of balancing in a yoga pose and know that a moment of relief and perspective is only a few breaths away. Just as each yoga pose takes a certain amount of strength and flexibility, so too does each step on your wedding day. Just as you must find a new alignment and balance with each new yoga pose, so too will you need to find equilibrium at each stage of the day as you transition from make-up to pictures to the aisle. And just as you can take a rest in yoga and sit still in baby pose, so too must you remember that it is your wedding day, and you can always take a moment to pause and check in with yourself.

You may not be a singer or a yogi, but you no doubt have a place in life where you really trust yourself—a place where you can be present without doubt or judgment. Rely upon this metaphorical anchor on the big day, and even if you get dropped to the floor on your first dance, you will know the way to that place of inner balance and calm.

Chapter Seven
After the Fanfare: Post-Wedding Blues

CHAPTER CONTENTS:

Married and I Can't Get Up
What Goes Up Must Come Down
What Do I Do With My Time Now?
What is This Thing Called Marriage?

It's A Wrap

MARRIED AND I CAN'T GET UP

You may see the title to this chapter and quickly skip past it, closing the book, figuring that you will read it later. In fact, it probably seems like an impossibility that you will even *need* to read this chapter. After all, after the wedding, not only will you be done with all of the annoyances of planning, but you will be high on the memories and enthralled by all that the future holds.

But don't shut the book just yet and ride off into your sunset. Read on, as you may need to recall this information when, after your wedding, you feel like things are just not right. You may feel blissful, everything having gone perfectly, but you may feel stuck in moving on. Or perhaps the reality of what it means to be married

has set in, and you feel sad that there is no more uncertainty in this realm. You have chosen your partner
for life, and now there is no more courting, dating, and
wondering. It can feel quite depressing, even if intellectually it is not.

✧ ✧ ✧

Yasmine and Jack jetted off to Mexico for their
honeymoon. On the airplane, they were all giggles,
sitting up in first class for the first time in their lives
and enjoying all the attention that honeymooners
get. Together they recounted funny and memorable
parts of the wedding, and both felt as if they were
riding a "high."

However, within days, Yasmine's elation was
mixed with some post-wedding anxiety. She regretted that she hadn't included her brother more in
the wedding and felt a shudder of embarrassment
every time she thought about what she said during
her toast. Jack tried to console her, yet it did not always ease her disappointments in herself. Not wanting these regrets to rule her honeymoon, she tried
to direct her attention to Jack and to enjoy this time
alone with one other before heading back to work
and the demands of life and home.

Most of the time in Mexico was complete bliss.
Yet, Yasmine, normally very level-headed, couldn't
help being quite snappy at Jack. She barked at him for
always insisting on being tour director, for taking pictures of everything that they saw, and belittled him
for not smelling better in the morning when waking
up. Yasmine intellectually knew she was struggling

with the magnitude of what being married means—that all these things were things she had to deal with "forever."

Yasmine was quite self-aware and managed to swing back into her norm after some deep reflection and some perspective-gathering. After all, she loved being in a warm, sunny place with the man she loved (quirks and all), with nothing to do but just be together. No wedding planning, no family, just the two of them.

As they flew home, again in first class, they both felt a bit bummed out. They did not want this wonderful journey to end. Jack jokingly said, *"Since it's Friday tomorrow, let's do a second honeymoon somewhere?"* As she Googled some B&Bs up north from their home, she remembered thinking, *what a perfect way to transition home.*

✿ ✿ ✿

What Goes Up Must Come Down

In the months leading up to your wedding, you may have felt your body and mind kick into hyper-drive, internalizing the stress but using it as a motivator. There was always something new to do or something new to think about. The nervous excitement may have felt intoxicating.

But it is a law of nature that *what ever goes up must come down*. Like the moon and the seasons, our bodies, minds, and emotions cycle and shift. They ebb and flow. We often push ourselves like robots with only one speed: fast. Yet, there is no way you can keep that pace for the six months before your wedding without collapsing afterwards, either emotionally or physically. At some point, the wave you are riding is going to crash.

Crashing does not necessarily need to be perceived in a negative light. It is natural and normal to feel down, depressed, and lethargic after a period of elation, excitement, and mania. These down days following your wedding may not feel as fun as darting around high as a kite, but they are restorative both physically and emotionally.

There is no reason to feel blue or ashamed about your need to rest. Your energy and mood are low for a reason. Your body and mind are exhausted. You need a break. You may even get sick almost immediately after. Your body has been maxed out and it is crying for a rest.

But have you ever thought, *"It was so nice to get sick. I finally had an excuse to sleep in and take care of myself."* Why not use this time as an opportunity to take care of yourself as if you were sick? Take a nap after work. Say no to a few social engagements. Sleep in on the weekend. Go home early. Take a sick day. Cancel plans to attend the wedding of your second cousin. Make every night a movie night.

It is understandable that slowing down after six months of mania may feel odd or strange; it may even induce guilt that you are being lazy. However, if you resist the crash, you may notice even more discomfort. The more you accept this period of "blah" sluggishness as a normal and natural part of the wedding process, the more you can enjoy it and use it as an excuse to indulge yourself a bit.

What Do I Do With My Time Now?

Probably the most common (and benign) let-down experience is in not knowing what to do with all your time now. You may feel as if you have completely lost touch with old interests, your bridal identity being all that you can recall. You can't even remember what you used to do to fill a whole Saturday now that you don't have a To-Do list three pages long.

This may feel a bit depressing (and even embarrassing), but it is an easy fix, and one that just requires a little energy once you have adequately restored your reserves. Dust off that tennis racket, pick up your knitting needles, rejoin your book club, plan weekly lunches with colleagues and friends. Engage in familiar activities and with familiar people who will not only restore you emotionally but will also help in restoring your pre-bride identity that probably feels a bit lost and out at sea.

What Is This Thing Called Marriage?

Perhaps the idea of being a "wife" is a role you have aspired to become your entire life and you feel right at home now. Or maybe you feel totally bizarre to actually be a "wife"; just saying the word gives you the creeps, conjuring up all sorts of thoughts about endless laundry and dishes. Regardless, adjusting to marriage is not always a cakewalk.

Now that the honeymoon is literally over, you may find yourself shocked to find out that your fiancé (now husband!) still snores, watches sports 24/7, and leaves his socks on the floor. You may even have a heightened level of irritation over those things that you ignored dur-

169

ing the engagement bliss. The realization that you are now married feels tremendous. You may have romanticized what this transition would look like, and it feels nothing like what you expected. Talk about letdown!

On the other hand, marriage may not feel that different from what it was before. Perhaps you were already living together or had been dating for many years. This *lack of change* in itself could also feel like a letdown, even if it is warmly familiar. But rest assured, you will indeed notice a change at some point. You just may not feel the shift until something actually tests you—kids, a big fight, sharing the holidays—something clearly signifying that you are now officially husband and wife.

No matter how you are feeling post-wedding bells, call on your Bridal Buddha. Your feelings of shock, disappointment, or irritation are just part of transitioning and adjusting. Take a step back, and give yourself and your new marriage a little time to readjust.

✿ ✿ ✿

Be Mindful of Depression

In this post-wedding phase, it's important to differentiate between what feels like a reasonable disappointment versus what may feel a bit like depression. If for a prolonged period of time you notice you are unable to function or enjoy activities you normally find pleasurable, definitely reach out to family, friends, a mentor or a psychotherapist. Nipping depression in the bud is crucial. The longer you let negative thought patterns persist, the longer it will take to shift them, and the more you may retreat from your life and your marriage. Do not let it drag on too long before you get help.

✿   ✿   ✿

IT'S A WRAP

As soon as he popped the question you may have discovered that being engaged was not what you thought it would be like. From the outside, being engaged may have looked like a beautiful shiny new diamond ring. Yet up close, those of us who have walked down that aisle and have worn that diamond ring know that there are more things to see when you look closer. Yes, it can be a stunning and wonderful experience, but it is not perfect.

If you are reading these last paragraphs, congratulate yourself. You have taken some extra time (despite being stretched so thin) to look closer: at that ring, within yourself, and all around you. You are allowing the Bridal Buddha to be born. We realize this may sound corny, but most people don't take the time to grow from this special rite of passage.

Each bride has her own unique challenges. Whether it was the endless process of planning, managing the relationships that surrounded you, understanding your identity, centering yourself on your wedding day or managing the post-wedding blues, *unveiling your wedding takes courage.*

POSTSCRIPT

We thank you for listening to our stories and our advice. We wrote this with the hope to not only help you through your engagement but to also more importantly allow you to gain insights in your life that you can hold onto forever. On a sociopolitical level, we hope our country will start having a deeper understanding of the realities of a modern bride and find new ways to support these women.

As authors, we have been engaged (sorry for the pun!) in writing this book for years. It has been truly a labor of love. We genuinely hope it helps you. Please be in contact with us. We would love to hear what helps you, your stories, what advice you have to offer other brides and how you personally unveiled your wedding.

Congratulations!

Cheers,
Rebecca & Tasha
www.unveilingweddings.com

ACKNOWLEDGEMENTS

Although our names are on the cover, it took a community of talented and creative professionals, friends, and family to create this book. We are grateful to all of you for your support and guidance over the years.

A special thank you to Brittany Olsen, our first editor, for assisting us in finding our voice and for making our ideas about brides and their journey shine. We are so appreciative of your vision and how you helped us restructure and organize our book. You are not only a great editor, but also a talented psychotherapist as well as a supportive and thoughtful friend.

Additionally, we are so grateful to Jean Taylor, our second editor. You have an amazing eye for detail, worked at lighting speed and polished this book as if was your own.

To Angela Rinaldi our agent, you saw something in this book before we had written a word of it. While you never sugarcoated how difficult publishing could be, you believed in *Unveiling Weddings* and gave us encouragement we needed to get this dream of ours into print. Additionally, you were very generous with your time, treated us with utmost respect, and looked out for our best interest. Thank you.

Thank you to Rafael Bernardino, our lawyer at the law firm of Bassi, Edlin, Huie, and Blum. We are appreciative of your expertise and your generousity of time.

We are especially indebted to our brides for your stories and insights. Your descriptive narratives gave our book depth, and we are forever grateful for your contributions. Our hope is that brides will no longer feel as isolated and alone in their wedding journey after reading about the wonderful highs and devastating lows of your experiences. Also we want to make a very special thank you to our early readers, Rebecca Jackson and Lauren Basham, who were willing to read really some *very* rough drafts and provide us with honest feedback, while at the same time keeping us excited about moving forward.

To our husbands, Tod and John, thank you for everything. *Unveiling Weddings* was a labor of love, and you supported us every step of the way. Thank you for believing in us. We are forever grateful.

Thank you.

APPENDIX

Brach, Tara, *Radical Acceptance*. New York, New York: Bantam Dell, 2003.

Chapman, Gary, *The 5 Languages of Love*. United States of America: Zondervan Bible Publishers, 1995.

Donohue, J. (2006, March). *The Transfigurative Power of the Imagination*. Speech presented at Psychotherapy Networker Symposium - The Creative Leap, Washington, DC.

Gottman, John, *The Seven Principles for Making Marriage Work*. New York: Three Rivers, 1999.

Hanh, Thich Naht, *Peace is Every Step: The Path of Mindfulness in Everyday Life*. New York, New York: Bantam Books, 1991.

Kingma, Daphne Rose, *Coming Apart: Why Relationship End & How To Live Through the Ending of Yours*. York Beach, ME: Conari Press, 2000. 1-800-423-7087

Linehan, Marsha M., *Cognitive-Behavioral Treatment of Borderline Personality Disorder*. New York, New York: The Guildford Press, 1993.

Linehan, Marsha M., *Skills Training Manual for Treating Borderline Personality Disorder*. New York, New York: Guilford Press, 1993.

Schwartz, Jeffery M., & Beyette, Beverly. *Brain Lock: Free Yourself from Obsessive-Compulsive Behavior*. Harper Perennial: New York, New York, 1997.

TASHA JACKSON FITZGERALD, MA, is a marriage family therapist who works in private practice. She is interested in helping people take a journey within themselves by learning from their relationships. Tasha has a particular interest in helping support women through important times of transition. She has been influenced by her MA in Counseling Psychology, specialized training in DBT, which is a combination of Zen philosophy and Western thinking, as well as her travels around the globe. Tasha resides in San Francisco with her husband and daughter.

REBECCCA SACERDOTI, PHD is a clinical psychologist who has experience working a variety of settings, including private practice, agency work and in schools. Her research experience stems from time spent working at the Department of Psychiatry at Stanford University. Currently, she has a private practice in San Francisco and she specializes in working with teens, adults and couples experiencing significant life changes. She sees psychotherapy as an opportunity to build inner balance, strength, and clarity in the face of the challenges that times of transition invite.